Moment
in
Time

by

Tom Polet

2010

"This is the day that the Lord has made;
We will rejoice and be glad in it."

Psalm 118:24

"This time, like all time, is a good time,
If we but know what to do with it."

Ralph Waldo Emerson

Written by:

Tom Polet

First Edition   Spring 2010

Author can be contacted in writing:

Tom Polet
143 West 31st Street
Holland, MI 49423

ISBN 978-0-557-33453-7

3

Acknowledgements

This has been an interesting book for me to write – a journey if you will. I have discovered with pleasure that when I seek to understand others more fully, I also learn things about myself.

So it has been with this book. I've learned that it's difficult to define anything, let alone time with complete accuracy and precision. All things are subject to interpretation as well as measurement error. And so on one hand, I leave this work less certain of what "A Moment In Time" looks like than ever before. And on the other, I am delighted that I have a much broader definition, and understanding of that elusive thing we call "time."

I want to thank all of my friends that were willing to expose significant truths and vulnerable areas of their lives for examination. That takes courage and trust that the fruits of that exposure will positively impact others in the name of Christ. We are called in Mark 15 to "spread the gospel," and so we do that individually, collectively, and uniquely, as these small vignettes demonstrate.

It's a good thing we can't see very far in front of us, or often times we would never venture down the road that brings us to Christ. And thank God that he *can* see in front of us. It's what makes conversion and salvation possible; all in "A Moment In Time."

T.P.
March, 2010

Index

Forward

The idea for this book had its roots from a conversation I was having with my friend Bruce up at his cabin in Northern Michigan. We were sitting on the deck looking over Lake Maramichi on an early summer day reviewing some things as it related to our accountability relationship.

During the course of that discussion Bruce read some passages out of 2nd Corinthians and 2nd Timothy, in effect commissioning me to take what I had been learning from him and others in 12 step recovery, and using it to make a difference in others lives.

In Second Corinthians 5, Paul urges us to be about the business of reconciliation with God, in fact he tells us in chapter 5: verses 17-21 the following:

"Therefore, if anyone is in Christ, he is a new creation; the old is gone, the new has come! All of this is from God, who reconciled us to himself through Christ and gave us the ministry of reconciliation: that God was reconciling the world to himself in Christ, not counting men's sins against them. And he has committed to us the message of reconciliation. We are therefore Christ's ambassadors, as though God were making his appeal through us. We implore you on Christ's behalf: Be reconciled to God. God made him who had no sin to be sin for us, so that we might become the righteousness of God."

And in Second Timothy 4: verses 1-2 he writes:

" In the presence of God and of Christ Jesus, who will judge the living and the dead, and in view of his appearing and his

kingdom, I give you this charge: Preach the Word; be prepared in season and out of season; correct, rebuke and encourage – with great patience and careful instruction.

As we reviewed those scripture passages, I saw with some clarity for perhaps the first time that we are all called to be Christ's ambassadors, so the question for me was; what will I do with that charge?

I am a recovering alcoholic, and Bruce has spent a lot of time with me as a sponsor and a friend, working through those steps, and helping me to sort out how to apply them in my walk with Christ. And now, how to take that a step further.

He made a comment that really impacted me that day, and set me to thinking. He said, "You know Tom, we really don't get the chance to really influence all that many people in our lives – even if we travel in a pretty big circle, the people that we really can make an impact on is generally just a handful."

He continued, "If you think of yourself as a point on a large circle, and the people in your circle is your world, those are the people that are within a degree of yourself. Those then are the ones we have the best opportunity to impact. And then they in turn can impact the ones within a degree of them."

"It takes time to build relationships and trust to the point where you can really speak into their lives, so you need to nurture those relationships with care."

We talked quite a bit about that principle that day, and have revisited it since. I've thought about breakthrough moments in my own life where the influence of Bruce, and many others jelled together that I made a decision to make a *change in direction.* A decision to walk down a different path. How many moments like that have I had? How many different paths? Will there be more? In hindsight (or foresight) can I even articulate it? Were their multiple pivotal moments, or does just one stand out? Did that moment span a long length of time, or did something change quickly, a Damascus road conversion like the Apostle Paul. These thoughts have intrigued me.

As I've processed that, I've wondered about the other people in my life that I know well. What was it like for them? Or can they even relate to what I'm talking about?

So I thought, what if I interview people whom I know quite well and have a view of their lives that is at least somewhat intimate; what kind of doors will I open up if I ask them leading questions (if they will let me), and what should I be asking that will really expose the truth about an individuals comfort level with who they are. Because that's one of my fundamental questions: "Am I, are you, comfortable with who you are? Do I feel a need for change? Should I change whether I feel I should or not?" That of course leads to a lot of other questions: your faith, relationships, work, health, opportunity, circumstances, choices, goals – the list goes on.

As I've processed what Bruce shared with me that day, and my thoughts on the subject since, I've realized I have choices to make. Turn left or right, go forward or sideways, go up or down. What I mean by that is this; what should I do with the insight (however limited it may be) that I've gained through recovery, and my spiritual journey? Do I have a responsibility to share that even though my circle of influence may be pretty small?

I believe the answer is yes. And so I am intentionally trying to do that in my interaction with those that cross my path, as well as those that may choose to read some of the things I have written. Time will tell if intention meets reality. That's what this book is about. The people in the following pages have given me permission to interview them and print my observations. In addition, I've explored the lives of some pretty famous people, and have included either things they said about themselves, or observations made by myself and other biographers.

The attempt then, is to tie the three concepts and observations together; defining the moment in time for individuals, looking to see if they were satisfied with who they were, and who they became, and how one persons change effected others; the power of influence, and in particular when I can show the correlation between different individuals here within this book.

So we have some famous people, and people from my everyday walk of life. Some are who I say they are, some are anonymous. But in the interviewing and recording I've learned more about myself, and I believe the people I interviewed and subsequently shared with have learned something also. So it's worth the effort. I hope you find this as interesting to read as I found it to write.

My Grandfathers Clock

by
Henry Clay Work

My grandfathers clock
Was to large for the shelf,
So it stood ninety years on the floor;
It was taller by half
Than the old man himself,
Though it weighed not a pennyweight more.
It was bought on the morn
Of the day that he was born,
It was always his treasure and pride;
But it stopped – short
Never to go again,
When the old – man died.

Ninety years without slumbering,
Tick, tock, tick,
His life seconds numbering
Tick, tock, tick.
And it stopped short
Never to go again,
When the old man died.

In watching its pendulum
Swing to and fro,
Many hours had he spent while a boy;
And in childhood and manhood
The clock seemed to know,
And share both his grief and his joy.
And it struck twenty – four

When he entered at the door,
With a blooming and beautiful bride;
But it stopped – short
Never to go again,
When the old – man died.

My grandfather said
That of those he could hire,
Not a servant so faithful he found;
For it wasted no time,
And it had but one desire,
At the close of each week to be wound.
And it kept in it's place,
Not a frown upon it's face,
And its hand never hung by its side.
But it stopped – short
Never to go again,
When the old – man died.

Well it rang an alarm
In the dead of the night,
An alarm that for years had been dumb;
And we knew that his spirit
Was pluming his flight,
That his hour of departure had come.
Still the clock kept the time,
With a soft and muffled chime,
As we silently stood by his side.
But it stopped – short
Never to go again,
When the old – man died.

Ninety years without slumbering,
Tick, tock, tick

His life seconds numbering,
Tic, tock ,tick
Well it stopped – short
Never to go again,
When the old – man died.

Chapter 1

"What is a Moment?"

"Little drops of water, little grains of sand,
Make the mighty ocean, and the pleasant land.
So the little minutes, humble though they be,
Make the mighty ages, of eternity."

by
Julia Carney

"Wait a minute. Now wait just a dog-gone minute. I'll be with you in a flash. You just hold your pants on and I'll be right there!"

Any idea how long it's going to take for the author of that sentence to do whatever he / she said they are going to do? It seems like it will happen almost anytime now, but by the way the sentence was phrased, you get the impression that the recipient is already impatient for whatever is supposed to be happening.

I can imagine an impatient ticket holder waiting to get in the gate. Or perhaps you are on hold for what seems like forever, and you're just trying to get a simple answer from a customer service representative.

What exactly is a moment? Wikipedia, defines it as "A brief, unspecified amount of time, or, the smallest portion of time."

Which is it? An unspecified amount of time could be a day, a year, or a lifetime. The smallest portion of time is; what?

14

In Psalm 90: 4 it says; "For a thousand years in your sight (the Lords) are like a day that has just gone by." If we take that literally (shouldn't we?) then it's not a very big stretch to say that a moment could be about anything!

There was a blog on the internet that I visited that asked that very question: and of course, it received a multitude of different definitions. Here are just a few:

- The time it takes for quark to become anti-matter
- The instant the measurement is taken
- ½ the length of a piece of string
- There are 67 instants in a moment
- A moment is 3 nano seconds
- It's relative to the subject or the company you are keeping
- It's too bloody soon – I wasn't ready

Abbot and Costello would have had a field day;

A. What am I looking at?
C. You're looking at now – everything is now
A. What happened to then?
C. We passed it.
A. When?
C. Just now – we are at "now" – now.
A. Let's go back to then.
C. When?
A. Now!
C. Now!?
A. Yes, now!
C. I can't
A. Why?
C. We missed it.

A. When?

C. Just now.

A. Well, when will then be now?

C. Soon.

A. How soon?

C. Right after when!

A friend of mine once commented that; "time *may* be quantified, but to do so, you need to establish absolute position." Hmmm.

I love this one: Another friend said; "A moment is what it might take to finish what he started, but an instant is what it takes to remove his clothes when his wife suggests sex."

And finally, instant oatmeal takes a couple of minutes to make.

<>

The song, *"My Grandfathers Clock,"* that I included in the couple of pages preceding this chapter, shows time starting and stopping when a person enters this world, and then when they leave it. Nothing could be further from the truth. The fact is that time marches on, with us or without us.

Would it not be sad if at the point of our leaving this mortal world, the clock of our life stopped right there, and the event of us being here, or not being here, made no difference at all?

And so while true that our mortal bodies are here for a finite period of time, the fact is the *impact* of our life here in this finite realm can transcend those time and space constraints, and *will* if we are intentional about our journey.

<>

Well, back to the subject of time. It seems that we have some liberty in our definition of "a moment in time." And again, for the purpose of this book we define it as that "period of awakening and change" that has occurred in our lives to bring us to where we are today. We are just a sojourner at a mile marker, on the road of time.

Chapter 2

" My Dad"

Tell me not, in mournful numbers,
Life is but an empty dream!
For the soul is dead that slumbers,
Things are not, what they seem.

Life is real! Life is earnest!
And the grave is not its goal;
Dust thou art, to dust returnest,
Was not spoken of the soul.

Not enjoyment, and not sorrow,
Is our destined end or way;
But to act, that each tomorrow
Finds us further than today.

Art is long, and time is fleeting,
And our hearts, though stout and brave,
Still, like muffled drums are beating
Funeral marches to the grave.

In the worlds broad field of battle,
In the bivouac of life,
Be not like dumb driven cattle!
Be a hero in the strife!

Trust no future, however pleasant!
Let the past, bury it's dead!
Act! Act in the living present!
Heart within, and God o'erhead!

Lives of great men all remind us,
We can make our lives sublime,
And departing, leave behind us
Footprints on the sands of time;

Footprints, that perhaps another,
Sailing over life's domain,
A forlorn and shipwrecked brother,
Seeing, shall take heart again.

Let us then be up and doing,
With a heart for any fate;
Still achieving, still pursuing,
Learn to labor and to wait.

"A Psalm of Life"

by
Henry Wadsworth Longfellow
1838

A vignette is a short story: a snip of a greater, bigger tale, that hopefully captures the essence of the story line the author is trying to deliver. It can be a written story, or perhaps a short film, or even a brief play. The idea is to keep it brief enough that it can be absorbed in one setting; perhaps a bus ride, or a lunch break, or a few minutes before turning the lights out at night. It's particularly nice when you can tie one story to another, to another. That is something I am trying to do here.

My Dad was influenced by other people that I am writing short stories about. Vignettes if you will. Christ, the Apostle Paul, Martin Luther, all played a role in shaping who my Dad

19

became. He of course, shaped me. And so as you read the story about him, and the subsequent stories, play the connections out in your mind. It becomes easy to see how much influence we all have if we are intentional about it. And sometimes unintentionally. Regardless, without further introduction: my Dad.

My Dad (James Polet) was born in Steins, Friesland, the Netherlands, July 22, 1929. He was the third oldest child in a family that would have seven boys and two girls.

His world, especially before World War 2 was pretty small, everything was pretty much confined to the small community he lived in. And of course, this was a day and age when information from outside of the community was by in large limited to what you read in books or learned in the classroom, or perhaps from the pulpit.

I sat down with my Dad recently and I told him I wanted him to articulate to the best of his ability the moment in time he knew that Jesus was Lord of his life. Not only Lord of his life, but how he came to that understanding. Was there a point that he realized that he didn't understand it quite the same any more? For better or for worse? What did he do with that realization? Did he stuff it and ignore it? Or did he explore the paradigm change that had taken place and try to figure out how then he should change as well? Is there anybody that really goes through that sort of introspective thinking – or deeper? Did he, do we, examine our faith at its fundamental core? And if we do, is it a catalyst for actual change in our behaviors and attitudes? I think these are big questions that seldom get talked about, yet they should, shouldn't they?

<>

God, Jesus Christ, church, and doctrine were all interwoven into the fabric of my Dad's life from as early as he can remember. Listen to my Dad reminisce in his own words:

"When I was a young boy growing up, God wasn't so much talked about as he was assumed. God was as much a part of our life as breathing. He was there. When I was a kid, my Dad continued, my father was the cornerstone for spiritual leadership in the home. Meals started and ended with prayer and a Bible reading, mostly Old Testament, and it was unheard of to talk about Jesus in the context of having a personal relationship with him. God was God, Jesus was Jesus, and faith and Christian living was always talked about from the context of covenant. This is how I grew up."

"Furthermore, there were clear distinctions between Christians and non-Christians, both explicate and assumed. My Dad explained. Christians had to go to the Christian school, and heathens went to public schools! So there was a clear class distinction between believers and unbelievers."

"Starting in the first grade there was Bible reading, verse memorization, and story telling. In particular from the Old Testament, and so the truth of the covenant; creation, fall, redemption, and restoration was drilled deeply into us from as soon as we were able to comprehend."

My Dad started to warm up to his subject – (truth be told it never takes him very long). "And then at age 12, I joined the young peoples society at church, just like everyone else, he continued, It was two hours once a week with two essays that you would have to write and share. The first hour was a

Biblical topic that the teacher chose and the second hour was one of your own choosing. Usually it was politics, or social and economic issues. So from an early age, faith was intertwined with politics, and economics, social and political justice. For me, that was as natural as natural can be!" Dad exclaimed, "and then you have to remember, when I was 12, it was the start of World War 2 and we were under Nazi occupation for 4 long years: the injustice and atrocities we saw and heard about, further honed my zeal for seeking the opposite! Justice, equity and God's promises became paramount. And that shaped who I was and who I would remain to be throughout my life!" he said with emotion.

As I listened to Dad, and interjected his dialogue with questions, I started to see a bit more clearly what drove him to be who I knew him to be. The man he was, and the man he is today.

And so my Dad grew into early adulthood with a clear sense in his own mind of what was right and what was wrong. In fact you might even say he was a zealot in his beliefs. Early adulthood also saw him immigrating into Canada with his family and then later into the USA with my mother, my two sisters, and myself. In each of these significant events, the church became the vehicle in which adjustment into the local society occurred. Canada was a bitter experience for both my Dad and Mom, and they saw the USA as a place where they could make a life for themselves and their children. The fact that there was Christian education in Holland Michigan played a major role in their decision to immigrate there. In their eyes it was the covenantal responsibility they had as it related to their kids education and upbringing.

But for a man who had the passion and energy to try and influence change, a simple life was not nearly enough. And Dad had that passion, and also a strong belief in the ideology that had it's core rooted in his upbringing. And so he threw himself into causes: in the early years it was Citizens for Educational Freedom, state and local politics – as he got older his zeal for justice and equity caused him to spend tireless hours with organizations such as the Association for Public Justice and the National Association for Christian Political Action. And fundamentally through these years his definition of faith and covenant never really changed. For him "faith" meant a vision of who God is and how he works through history and the events that happen. It meant that Jesus was an event that happened because God promised it would – and God fulfills his promises so he may be known.

My Dad took a breath and I took the opportunity to ask him my big question; "So Dad, I said. What changed? You are not the same man today that you were all those years when I was growing up. Your tenacity to issues and in particular to doctrine are much more open and relaxed then they ever were. Not that I'm complaining; I like it, but why?"

Dad responded. "When I went into retirement, I wanted to stay active, and I found that Habitat for Humanity and Jubilee Ministries fit well into what I desired to do: give to those who had a need, and to stay physically active as well."

"A surprising and delightful byproduct was the fact that as I worked with fellows from different walks of life, I found myself really enjoying the interchange of ideas. Especially as it related to faith, politics, social and economic justice. After all, these were my life's passions. I'm not exactly sure why I became so much more open to other ideas and thoughts;

partially it was because of the different reading I began to expose myself to. Perhaps it was because the pace of my life was much less hectic and I had a chance to reflect more, or perhaps it was because I started to see that a one-sided point of view didn't work; regardless, I became much more receptive to other interpretations of faith and who God is."

We both agreed that it was the height of arrogance to think that the Christian Reformed community had the corner on religious truth and thought. I complimented my Dad on the changes that I had the pleasure to observe in the last number of years. I also complimented him on the fact that he was and is a man that will stand up for what he thinks is right. But he also is now a man that allows himself to be teachable.

My Dad has made a difference. In the lives of his children, his wife, his extended family, and his community. His love of God is unquestioned. His faith in God's goodness has never wavered. He is a man that has worked to live his life as God commands to the best of his ability, and in doing so, he has made those around him better people. And now at the age of eighty, when most have stopped wanting to learn and explore new thoughts, Dad is still keenly interested in seeing what God reveals to him next. And in that process, he continues to have Christ grow in and through him. What more could you ask or want?

Chapter 3

"The Apostle Paul"

Fly, envious time, till thou run out thy race;
Call on the lazy leaden – stepping hours,
Whose speed is but the heavy plummet's pace;
And glut thyself with what thy womb devours,
Which is no more than what is false and vain,
And merely mortal dross;
So little is our loss,
So little is thy gain.
For when, as each thing bad thou hast entomb'd
And last of all thy greedy self consumed,
Then long eternity shall greet our bliss,
With an individual kiss;
And joy shall overtake us, as a flood,
When everything that is sincerely good,
And perfectly divine,
With truth, and peace, and love, shall ever shine,
About the supreme throne
Of him, to whose happy-making sight, alone,
When once our heavenly-guided soul shall climb,
Then all this earthly grossness quit,
Attired with stars, we shall forever sit,
Triumphing over death, and chance,
And thee! O time!

"On Time"

by
John Milton

So who exactly was the Apostle Paul? Not one of Christ's 12 disciples, he called himself the "The Apostle to the Gentiles," and, along with Peter and James, was the most notable of the early Christian missionaries.

When we are first introduced to Paul, he is Saul of Tarsus, in a scene that is both brutal and bloody. He is present at the stoning of Stephan, the young, zealous Christian that was stoned by the *Sanhedrin* because of his stand for Christ. Acts 7 & 8 tells of Saul "standing in hearty agreement with putting him to death," and in fact, he held the robes of the executioners.

Who is this man? He was a Jew, from the city of Tarsus in Cilicia, some 250 mile northwest of Jerusalem, a few miles inland from the Mediterranean Sea, a place which today is part of Turkey. Because the city was near a seaport, it became a popular trade route for caravans carrying their goods from the Orient in the east, all the way to Rome in the west.

He was a man whom at a young age was well versed in the laws of the Jews, and went to on to become a strong member of that ruling class – a passionate, determined, Pharisee – probably with ambitions of serving on the ruling *Sanhedrin* council. Look at his own words from 1 Timothy 1:12-13 "I thank Christ Jesus our Lord, who has strengthened me, because he considered me faithful, putting me into service: even though I was formerly a *blasphemer, and a persecutor, and a violent aggressor.* And yet I was shown mercy because I acted in unbelief." How's that for telling on yourself!

In Charles Swindoll's book "A Man of Grace and Grit – Paul" he makes three poignant observations of the young man that Paul was; good things for all of us to remember.

1. No matter how you appear to others today, everyone has a dark side.
2. Regardless of what you have done, no one is beyond hope.
3. Even though your past is soiled, everyone can find a new beginning with God.

Let's go back in time. If you look in the ninth book of Acts you will see that the reason for Saul traveling to Damascus, was to round up "Christ followers," and bring them back to Jerusalem. He was on a mission! You could even say he was obsessed with the idea of purging Christianity in any manner he knew how.

According to Acts, his conversion takes place on that road to Damascus, where he experienced a vision of the resurrected Christ, after which he was temporarily blinded. Literally, God spoke from the heavens to him and said; "Saul, Saul, why are you persecuting me?" (Acts 9:3-4) God intervened in the life of Saul at the moment when it would have its greatest impact – he intervened at a point when Saul was out of control!

Is that not true for a lot of us? A point in our life where we don't know which way to turn; the loss of a child, a bad health diagnose, loss of a job, an addiction that has your life spiraling downwards; you know what I mean, God shows up when you least expect it. At a point when he believed you were ready to listen. The question is; will you?

Paul never actually met Jesus. He asserted that he received the Gospel not from man, but through the revelation of the Holy Spirit.

He *did* however, develop a relationship with some of Christ's disciples, but it was a full three years after his conversion and baptism, and then only after the intercession of Barnabas. It was reasonable that the disciples would be wary of Paul because he was well known as an individual who was a persecutor of the church.

Regardless of all of that, we know that Paul spent time with both James and Simon Peter (Ref. Galatians 1:13-24), and it would not be overly presumptive to imagine that the teachings and miracles of Jesus were the main topic of conversation.

At least seven of the New Testament epistles are certainly Paul's, making him the most prolific New Testament writer. In addition, three others may have been written by him. Again, regardless of exactly how many were or were not, Paul's influence on Christian thinking arguably has been more significant than any other New Testament author. Most of his writing occurred in the time frame of 50 -62 AD, and much of it was a cornerstone for the doctrines of the Christian Church right from its infancy.

Paul was a driven man. This is a guy that extensively traveled during a time in history where travel wasn't very easy. He was confrontational to the point where he put his life in jeopardy several times. He was hunted by disgruntled Jews from Antioch and is stoned to the point where he was left for dead. He was imprisoned, tortured, you name it; yet he continued to carry the message.

And carry the message he did. He covered a much greater geographical area than Christ ever did, and seemed to be a guy that had his finger into everything. Some have even gone as far as saying that the advancement of Christianity owes as much to Paul as to Jesus.

One of the unique characteristics of Paul was the fact that there *was* such a diametrical change. And also his type AAA personality; once he embraced Christianity, he did it with heart, body, soul, and mind. He was on fire! His teachings and messages on grace have soothed and healed untold legions of men and women since they have been published. Yet he never could have taught that, if he had not experienced it! And he did! Who but Christ can wash away the guilt of some of the transgressions like Paul had done? No one – and he *knew it!*

For myself, Paul is the New Testament writer that makes the most sense. What I mean by that is this; his writings help me to articulate and define the whole essence of faith and obedience. There used to be a commercial on television about E.F. Hutton a stock firm whose slogan was; "When E.F. Hutton talks, people listen." Well for me, when I read Paul's letters; I start to get it. I start to have an understanding of "what then shall I do."

Take for example the book of Romans. Right at the very beginning of the book, he (Paul) indentifies himself as an emissary of Christ. As an individual that has been set aside by God to deliver the gospel message. And calling the people to whom he is delivering the message to *obedience* that is established by faith (Romans 1:5).

As he goes on in the book of Romans, Paul identifies his own depraved and sinful nature, helps us to identify ours, and then shows us the remarkable promise of grace through faith (reference Romans 7 and 8 in particular).

What he has done, at least for me, is to help articulate how that conversion process is even possible. When I take that in conjunction with a lot of other things that have influenced my walk in faith, a paradigm change begins to take place. For me, a painfully slow process, but a change none the less. More on that subject later.

Paul turned out to have a remarkable sphere of influence. Why is that? What qualified his letters, experiences, observations etc. to be used so exclusively by the early church? We certainly know today that there were other letters and different authors that wrote about Christ during the same time frame but did not have their work included in the Bible. And we know that it was men of God (the early church) that made the decision of what to include – or exclude. So there is a huge faith element that all of us are called to either except or reject: That the words of Paul, along with all the other books of the Bible that are included in the traditional text, are indeed the words that God willed to be included. This is no time to be on a fence; you either do believe, or you don't.

I don't think however that you have to ignore or dismiss rational dialogue or debate about the interpretation of text. I believe it's a healthy component of every individuals walk in faith. Having said that, I also believe that there is a strong faith component that we all should be ok with having a bit of mystery about it; why else call it faith?

Well, I'm not a Biblical scholar by any stretch of the imagination, so I won't even pretend to go much deeper than I already have into all of that, but there is a couple of things that are irrefutable; Paul's circle of influence was huge in it's time, and it has been ever since. Here was a guy that made a difference! And here was a guy that didn't just let his "moment in time" slip by without doing something about it; he recognized a need for change in how he thought and lived, and then he went about the business of doing so! Speaking from a purely human perspective, I'm sure it wasn't the easier, softer road for him to follow; as is clearly illustrated when you read the rest of his story.

The story of Paul before and especially after his conversion is remarkable for a number of reasons. God clearly took matters in his own hands with Paul. God didn't idly stand by while Paul was busy persecuting Christians. He came down, blinded him so that he might see. The timing was critical. Christianity needed a jumpstart, and God chose Paul to be the catalyst. At the perfect moment in time. The rest is history.

Chapter 4

"Pete"

"An event is not any more intrinsically intelligible or unintelligible because of the pace at which it moves. For a man who does not believe in a miracle, a slow miracle would be just as incredible as a swift one."

"The Everlasting Man"

by
G.K. Chesterton

Yogi Berra once told a friend that wanted directions to his house; "When you get to the fork in the road, take it!" For Yogi that made sense because both ways led to his house.

My friend Pete has a somewhat similar story from the standpoint that he just followed the natural roads as they came to him; mostly kind of intuitively choosing the path that seemed to make sense at the time, until coming to a place in life where he can't imagine life without Christ at its head.

He came from a home that saw his parents split up at a fairly young age, but yet they kept a civil relationship. With both parents living in the same town, Pete divided his growing years between his parents; Monday thru Thursday at Mom's, then Friday, Saturday, and Sunday at Dad's. Both of his parents came from strict religious backgrounds, one Catholic and one Baptist, but practicing faith, churchgoing, etc. was totally absent from Pete's childhood and adolescence. He really had no sense that he was missing something.

Pete was and still is one of those guys that fairly instinctively makes good choices. Never one to get in real trouble, he went on to college, got a job and got married. A life that was good, values that were fundamentally rooted in following the rules of society, life went on. Until his wife decided that she wasn't interesting in continuing in the marriage relationship. For the first time Pete found himself exploring his values and trying to understand what was wrong with him and/or his wife that would cause this. Some counseling ensued, but it didn't really bring any revelation; nor did it heal the relationship. Suddenly alone in a big city away from his roots, he found himself really getting introspective for the first time. What was important? Making a decision that family was, he moved back to West Michigan to restructure his life; following a road that seemed like the one to be on without a great deal of thought as to why.

And then life did what life does. Events happened that in retrospect can clearly be seen as doors or roads of opportunities, which we can't necessarily see at the time when we are in the middle of it. Pete's grandfather (his Dad's Dad) died, and wanting to be a good grandson to his grandmother, he began taking her to her church. It was a local Catholic Parish.

While doing so, he began to absorb some of what he was seeing and hearing, again without any big sudden change or even a cognizant recognition of what was happening; he was being exposed to Christ. After about six months, he stopped going with his Grandmother, but he had developed a relationship with a neighborhood couple that went to a local

Methodist Church. One day Pete asked if he could join them some Sunday, they said "sure," and he began to be exposed to a style of teaching and preaching that became much more personal. And Pete found himself drawn to it; again without a real conscious effort. While attending the Methodist Church, he discovered himself "turning over rocks," looking to further understand Christianity and finding a lot of things that made sense, and found his faith growing; in a steady progression of time.

And then he met a lady that would eventually become his wife and she was a practicing Christian. So he went to church with her, got his first Bible, got exposed to more and more and when Pete and Jan decided to get married in the church, he was asked if he was ready to make public confession of his faith. Driven not by an overwhelming decision of turning his life over to Christ, but rather being driven by the fact that it seemed like the *right thing,* and the responsible thing to do; Pete did. And then something interesting happened.

His new father-in-law told him; "Pete, what you did today is the single most important thing you have ever done, or ever will do in this life. More important then marriage, career, children, whatever; this is it." For the first time Pete really starting taking a hard look at his faith, and his relationship with Christ. In doing so he realized that he wanted more; to believe and understand at a deeper level, and so for the first time really, he began an active pursuit of God. And as all of us know who are children of God, when we make a decision to actively pursue him, he *runs* to us.

34

Today, some 12 -13 years later, Pete can't imagine his life without Christ at its center. A dedicated family man with three young children, he is active in his church, regularly attends Bible studies and other Christian centered events, takes courses to enrich his faith, and has fully integrated that life into his marriage, home, and work. What Pete doesn't know are things all of us don't know on this side of heaven. He certainly doesn't know his future and to what type of tests he may yet be subjected to. He certainly doesn't really know exactly how his present would be if he had not made the choice to become a Christ follower when he did. And he doesn't really know the impact he may be having on his sphere of influence as a result of that decision. We really can only hypothesize.

It certainly wouldn't be too big of a stretch to assume that the odds of all of his children becoming Christian would be greatly diminished if he hadn't have made those choices. And of course we have no idea how big a circle of influence one of his children might have. What if one of his children becomes the next great evangelist? And brings tens of thousands to Christ? Who are we to say that it's not possible?

Here is an illustration of a man, a good man, who became a better man. It happened because the Holy Spirit moves among us whether we realize it or not, it happened because Pete made some intentional choices, and it also happened because a lot of other people also made choices; some dramatic, some soft, before Pete ever made his choice; does all of that make sense?

And God orchestrates it all! Wow! When we ponder the vastness of creation, the depth and breadth of humanity, to think that he is doing intentional things in Pete's life, and yours, and mine; in all of humanity, it staggers my ability to totally comprehend. What a gift.

I'm glad to know Pete and call him a friend. He is another sojourner on the path of life, a person I can share part of that path with, and a man with whom God is not finished with yet.

Chapter 5

"St. Augustine"

"What then is time? If no one asks me, I know what it is. If I wish to explain it to him who asks, I do not know."

by
St. Augustine

Born in 354, in the small town of Tagaste, Africa (now Algeria), Augustine lived in the time of the growing ascendancy of the Christian Church, and the decline of the Roman Empire.

I don't think too many people in the world today know who he was, what he did, or why he is important. I'll admit that for myself, his best known work, *"The Confessions of St. Augustine,"* has been a difficult book for me to read. I have picked it up many times, only to put it down because I felt myself getting distracted. So why would I choose this individual that has been hard for me to read, lived so very long ago, and had a very difficult time being at peace in his relationship with God, to write about? Perhaps, because I see part of myself in him.

It is important to remember that his "Confessions" are one of the great literary works to have survived intact over the Centuries. That in and of itself is reason enough to at least take a look at it. It is by no means the only work of Augustine that has survived. In addition to *"The Confessions,"* he also penned: *"On Christian Doctrine, City of God, On Free Choice of the Will,"* but to name a few.

Literally, hundreds of his books, letters, and sermons have survived intact.

Augustine, lived a privileged life as a young man, and traveled in the finest circles and attended the finest schools. At an early age he dedicated his life to education and teaching, but he was not a Christian. At age thirty, Augustine had won the most visible academic chair in the Latin world, and was also a devout follower of Manichaeism.

The basic doctrine of Manichaeism was "salvation through knowledge," as opposed to Christianity which was full of mystery. Manichaeism professed to be a religion of pure reason, it purported to explain the origin, composition, and future of the universe, in short; it had an answer for everything.

So at age thirty, he became the professor of rhetoric for the imperial court at Milan. It was while at Milan, that Augustine's life changed. While there, already dissatisfied with holes he observed in Manichaeism doctrine, his Mother influenced, (some might say pressured) him to consider Christianity. Also during this time he was being influenced by friends, which included Ambrose, the Bishop of Milan, to consider Christianity as well.

It was the summer of 386 AD. After reading and account of Saint Anthony of the Desert which greatly inspired him, Augustine experienced "a moment in time," a moment like no other before, in which his life changed forever. It caused him to give up his career in rhetoric, quit his teaching position in Milan, give up any ideas of marriage, and convert to Christianity. From that point forward, he devoted himself entirely to serving God, the practices of priesthood, and celibacy.

Key to this conversion was a child-like voice he heard singing "take up and read," while he rested under a certain fig tree in a garden in Milan.

Augustine writes:

" I cast myself down, I know not how, under a certain fig tree, giving full vent to my tears; and the floods of mine eyes gushed out an acceptable sacrifice to Thee. And, not indeed in these words, yet to this purpose, spake I much unto thee: and Thou, O Lord, how long? How long Lord, wilt thou be angry forever? Remember not our former iniquities, for I felt I was held by them. I sent up these sorrowful words: How long, how long, tomorrow and tomorrow? Why not now? Why not is there this hour and end to my un-cleanliness?

So I was speaking and weeping in the most bitter contrition of my heart, when, lo! I heard from a neighboring house a voice, of a boy or girl, I know not, chanting, and oft repeating, "Take up and read' Take up and read." Instantly, my countenance altered, I began to think most intently whether children were wont in any kind of play to sing such words: nor could I ever remember ever to have heard the like. So checking the torrent of my tears, I arose; interpreting it to be no other than a command from God to open the book (the Bible), and read the first chapter I should find. "

So after hearing the child's voice, Augustine rushed to his house, and picked up a book written by the Apostle Paul to the Romans, opened it, and instantly read: (Romans 13:14-

14) *"Let us behave decently, as in the daytime, not in orgies and drunkenness, not in sexual immorality and debauchery, not in dissention and jealousy. Rather, cloth yourself with the Lord Jesus Christ, and do not think how to gratify the desires of the sinful nature."*

Augustine continued his narrative: *"No further would I read; nor need I: for instantly at the end of this sentence, by a light as it were of serenity infused into my heart, all the darkness of doubt vanished away."*

He was changed! At that moment, his life took a new direction. Granted, the preceding months and years had honed his dissatisfaction with the life he was leading, and with his understanding of God. But the point is he heard the voice of God, and he responded.

Augustine was an incredible thinker and teacher, and he would devote the balance of his life to those gifts. His insight and teachings have effected all of Christendom from that time forward.

He was also a man driven to try and understand the mysteries of the universe. As you read his "Confessions" and drink in his self examination, it is with a bit of irony that I observe his preoccupation with his inability to define "time." He devotes a good deal of his writing to the very subject. A few of those chapters are worth repeating, because it demonstrates how he, and we in our own intellect, can not make sense of God's divine plan.

Again, Augustine in his "Confessions" inquires into the nature of creation and time:

"Allow me Lord, to seek further. For if times past and future do exist, I want to know where they are. I realize that if I can not know this, that wherever they are, they are not there as future or past, but as present. For if there, also, they are future, they are not as yet there. If there, also, they are past, they are no longer there. Wherever they are, whatever they may be, they are only there as present."

Augustine searches for examples: *"Let me find some example from the abundance of such circumstances as I am thinking of. I see the daybreak. I foretell that the sun is about to rise. What I see is present. What I predict is future – not the sun, which already exists, but the sunrise, which is not yet. And yet, if I did not imagine the sunrise itself in my mind (as I do now while I speak of it), I could not foretell it. But the dawn which I see in the sky is not the sunrise, although it precedes it. Nor is that imagination in my mind the sunrise. Both of these things I see as present so that the other which is future may be foretold. Future things, then, are not yet, and if they are not as yet, they simply are not. And if they do not exist, they can not be seen at all. Yet they can be foretold from things present which already are, and are seen."*

Now Augustine exclaims his frustration and his dependence on God for answers to questions that he in his humanity can not answer. Again, from his confessions:

"And so, O ruler of your creation, how can you teach souls things to come? Certainly, you did teach your prophets. How do you, to whom nothing is future, teach things to come? Or rather, of future things, teach in the present? For what does not exist, certainly cannot be taught. This way of yours is to far from my view: it is to mighty for me, I cannot reach it, but

41

I will be enabled by __you,__ when you have granted it, O sweet light of my hidden eyes."

Can you imagine this man, who had grown up believing that there was an answer for everything, coming to the conclusion that time as we know it can not truly be defined? In a very real sense, his inability to put that question to rest, becomes one of the cornerstones for his subsequent faith in God. So in the end, even with his great intellect and his ability to solve complex problems and create order to abstract thoughts; he comes up empty. And acknowledges that on the one hand, we have God who clearly points the way to redemption and salvation and reveals that which he wishes to reveal, but on the other, does not allow us to fully comprehend time and space, the future, and the mystery and awe of serving a living, seen, yet unseen, Lord.

Augustine's sermons, teachings, and writings inspired another whole generation of individuals who carried the torch to the next, and then the next, in an ever widening circle. That circle of influence that we talked about early on, is still present for us today. He still influences men and women alike sixteen hundred years after his death. A man for all seasons. A man of God. A man who has stood the test of time.

Chapter 6

"Ken"

Two roads diverged in a yellow wood
And sorry I could not travel both
And be one traveler, long I stood
And looked down one as far as I could
To where it bent in the undergrowth

Then took the other as just as fair
And having perhaps the better claim
Because it was grassy and wanted wear
Though as for that, the passing there
Had worn them really the same

And both that morning equally lay
In leaves no step had trodden black
Oh, I kept the first for another day!
Yet, knowing how leads onto way
I doubted if I should ever come back

I shall be telling this with a sigh
Somewhere ages and ages hence
Two roads diverged in a wood
And I took the one less traveled by
And that has made all the difference

"A Road Less Traveled"

by
Robert Frost

Ken is a friend of mine. What a wonderful thing to say, and what a wonderful thing it is to know that here is a man that makes me a better man. It's great if you have a friend that is fun to be with, that's certainly a part of friendship, but when you have a friend that makes you a better person, now *that's* something special.

A somewhat typical West Michigander, Ken was born in 1952 to parents of Dutch Reformed background in Grand Rapids Michigan. Again, somewhat typically, a fairly large family (three boys, two girls), Church and Sunday school, and Christian Day School. When he was in seventh grade, his Dad bought a business in Holland Michigan and brought the family with him. Ken was the son that chose to follow his Dad into the business and learned it from the ground up.

West Michigan was and still is known for having a strong Reformed and Christian Reformed population. Back during the time Ken was going through adolescence, it was normal for boys and girls to make their public profession of faith when they were in about the 10th grade. When he decided not to do so, it began a period of rebellion against organized religion that was to last for several more years. His reasoning was simple. "I didn't see a change in people's behavior that did it. he told me, So I wasn't prepared to walk down that path just because I was expected to."

And so, even though that decision caused some heartache for his parents, he was resolute and lived a life that wasn't bad - but he wasn't saved.

Time passed as time does, high school graduation, college, a liberal sprinkling of living a carefree life, all within accepted social boundaries but without a well defined personal goal.

Other than work. Ken was a guy that did well at school, and after he was done, he came back to the family business of which he has run successfully now for many years. He has worked hard over that time to continue the tradition his father started: manage the business with honesty, integrity and excellence.

In February of 1973, his older brother Tom became a "born again" Christian, and rattled the family with that decision. Being "born again" was something foreign to reformed theology, your "right to salvation" was pre-ordained and not dependent on a "conversion." Something like that just didn't fit in the neat package of reformed thinking. Ken however, observed something genuine in Tom, which he didn't see in the people that had made confession of faith because it was expected. He saw a change, and Tom spoke of that change to him.

One day in October of 1974 Tom invited Ken to join him at his Bible study. Ken and he both had motorcycles at the time, and Ken was living in a cottage out by Lake Michigan. When they got to the corner of 152nd and Riley, Tom turned to his brother and asked again; "Do you want to come?" A left turn took Ken to the lake; a right turn would lead to the Bible study. Here it was; a moment in time whether he realized it or not, and he chose to go right, and *nothing* would ever be the same again. Sometimes, it's just that simple, and just that big all at the same moment.

When he got there that evening he met four couples who took the time to make Ken feel welcome and explain how Christ had change their lives. Those four men – Vern, Bill, Elmer, Bernie, and their wives would become a nucleus for Ken in the coming years as he made a decision to give his life to Christ. When he got back to his cottage that night, he fell to his knees and asked God to come into his life. The words of the prayer were not all that important: the condition and petition of his heart was everything.

What happened next is a story that has been repeated by so many that it almost seems hardly worth mentioning; and yet, it demonstrates how God is at work in our lives when we make an intentional choice to follow him. Shortly after his conversion Ken met Don, an older gentleman that took the time and effort to mentor Ken. To help prepare him for the road ahead, whatever that might hold. Ken continued in his journey with Don and his new friends and joined their Christian fellowship. It was a group of believers that followed Christ and sought to have him live in and through them.

Time moved forward, during the summer of 1980 his brother Tom was camping up in Ludington State Park and his dog and the dog of a neighboring camper got in a fight. Tom noticed that the neighbor had a bumper sticker on the car that said "Christians aren't perfect, just forgiven." A conversation ensued, it was discovered that this lady and her sister were both going to Hope College in Holland, it just so happened that Tom had a younger brother that really needed to meet a nice Christian girl; and of course you can guess the rest. Ken met Jean, and a year or so later in October of 1981 they got married, and the two became one.

It was a period of growth and normal responsibilities for Ken as he and Jean quickly started a family and settled into the business of life. A son and two daughters soon came and absorbed time and energy as children do. Jean and Ken certainly didn't ignore their faith or their desire to follow

Christ during all of this, but some chinks in the armor were developing in Ken's life without a cognizant realization that it was occurring.

Ken was busy with the responsibilities that are natural when you are leading a successful business, he was committed to his work and being a good leader. During the same time frame, his church fellowship disbanded, and Jean and Ken found themselves looking for a new church home. Busy with work, children, community and family activities, without realizing that it was actually even happening, the continued nurturing of their marriage intimacy was being neglected, as well as a constant re-evaluation of Kens own personal faith life.

All of a sudden, (we don't see it coming – do we) it's the late 1990's.Ken's business has grown to the point where he no longer feels he has the skill set to adequately lead it alone, so he's absorbed in that part of his life, the vocational frustration so many of us have to face: there's stress and a feeling of inadequacy, and the devil being who the devil is, he recognizes an opportunity and goes for the jugular.

It started out, oh so innocently, doesn't it most of the time? Checking out a couple of things on the internet, noticing a web site for the Sports Illustrated swim suit issue, a click here, a click there, and suddenly your viewing inappropriate material and you feel titillated and shame and guilt all at the same time. What happens when we keep that kind of stuff secret?

Well it doesn't usually get better. Now we have a secret that we are playing with and allowing to consume our energy and our ability to have a right relationship with God and the other people in our lives. Ken recognized that, but the male pride / ego thing kicked in and prevented him from laying it at Christ's feet and getting real with people about his struggle. So to medicate the shame and guilt, he viewed it more frequently, and began an inappropriate emotional relationship with another woman. And like a man drowning in the ocean with the life raft clearly in sight, he was sinking. Until he surrendered and allowed rescue to occur.

It's now February of 2003. The healing began with confession and repentance. Ken laid it all out for his wife and pledged to flee from that enemy. He sought out accountability. He wisely went to other men to talk about his problem and asked for help. He developed a support network. He committed time and effort and resources to Christian counseling for himself and his wife to bring healing. He took a hard look at the man in the mirror and made deliberate, intentional changes to help bring him closer to God, his wife and family, and his community. He recognized his need for help with his business to grow it to the next level, and put the right people in place to do that.

And mostly, he came before the Lord and acknowledged that in his own strength he was incapable of doing any of that. But with God's help, he could not only claim victory over his earthly "thorn in the flesh," he could also use it as a tool to further the kingdom of God.

As a direct result of that journey, Ken has intentionally helped create a couple of very important ministries in the local area. One of them is titled *Finishing Strong*. In my book with that very title name I talk about the group (which I am a part of) and the mission statement of:

1. Realizing the formation of Christ in us – Galatians 4:19
2. Realizing the transformation of our minds – Romans 12:1-2
3. Realizing the confirmation of us to become like Christ – Romans 8:29

Today, Ken's relationship with the Lord, his wife and family, and his circle of influence is as healthy as it has ever been, even more so. He has had some watershed moments: turn left or right, confess and repent. Or keep sinning, and drift on the sea. *Or* get intentional about a direction, and the fruit of that is being harvested in many people's lives. Ken has helped a number of men battle their addictions by sharing his story and participating in recovery related activities. He is active in mentoring several men individually. He leads and facilitates our *Finishing Strong* group. Ken has participated in the leadership and fellowship of a number of other recovery related activities in our community. He feels a strong calling to give of his experience, strength, hope and time to help men develop Godly lives. His heart today is wide open for God given opportunities to serve – *this* is what Christ meant when he said; "Follow me!"

It is a privilege for me and others to be able to stand along side Ken and intentionally work at becoming better men. I appreciate him, for the man he is, and the man he strives to be, a brother in Christ, fighting the good fight – one who is committed to: *Finishing Strong!*

Chapter 7

"Martin Luther"

A mighty fortress is our God,
A bulwark never failing;
Our helper he amid the flood
Of mortal ills prevailing.
For still our ancient foe
Doth seek to work us woe:
His craft and power are great,
And armed with cruel hate,
On earth is not his equal.

Did we in our own strength confide,
Our striving would be losing,
Where not the right man on our side,
The man of God's own choosing.
Dost ask who that may be?
Christ Jesus it is he;
Lord Sabbaoth, his name,
From age to age the same,
And he must win the battle.

And though this world with devils filled,
Should threaten to undo us,
We will not fear, for God hath willed,
His truth to triumph through us.
The prince of darkness grim,
We tremble not for him;
His rage we can endure,
For lo, his doom is sure;
One little word shall fell him.

That word above all earthly powers,
No thanks to them, abideth;
The spirit and the gifts are ours,
Thru him who with us sideth.
Let goods and kindred go,
This mortal life also;
The body they may kill;
God's truth abideth still;
His kingdom is forever.

"A Mighty Fortress"

by
Martin Luther

I was a young boy when I first heard this hymn. The organ in our church had all the stops pulled out and it was played at full blast with the pipes sounding like claps of thunder. It was dark, and heavy, and strong. The words and music echoed deep into my adolescence mind. My boyhood friend Sid Bruinsma and I would see how low we could make our voices go as we sang through the strong words of Martin Luther's classic Hymn; the battle of good versus evil. It still gives me shivers today when I hear it. I wish I would hear it more.

Who was this man? Born November 10, 1483 in Eisleben Germany, he was a German monk, theologian, university professor, and a church reformer whose ideas influenced Protestant reformation and greatly influenced the course of western civilization.

Those are pretty big labels and claims to put on one man; change the course of an entire civilization? How much influence can one man have?

Well he certainly had his share. Some of it was just simply being the right man in the right place at the right time. Being born and growing up in Germany during a time and place where lots of things were changing; in particular, the education of the common man. One of the major, if not *the* major reason why this was happing was because of the invention of the printing press by Johannes Gutenberg in the late 1430's. The natural result of that was putting books and manuscripts in the hands of more and more people than ever before in the history of mankind. It was only natural that the first things being printed were copies of the Bible. So by the time Luther came around some seventy years later, tradesmen and commoners alike were becoming literate for the first time in history in any significant numbers. What was happening to these people's minds as they gained knowledge was only natural; they wanted more, and they wanted explanations for the differences they saw in the Bible versus what they were being told from the pulpit. They were ripe for someone to come along and help aid them in their "reformational" thinking; enter, Martin Luther.

Luther's basic theology challenged the authority of the papacy (The Roman Catholic Church), and that the Bible was the only infallible source of religious authority. According to Luther, salvation was a gift of God, received only by true repentance and faith in Jesus as the Messiah, a faith *given* by God , and unmediated by the Church.

His translation of the Bible into the language of the people made the scriptures more accessible to them, and had tremendous political impact on the church and on German culture. It also furthered the development of a standard version of the German language, and influenced the translation of the English King James Version of the Bible. In addition, his hymns inspired the development of congregational singing in Christianity, all of this and more made him a remarkable man at a remarkable time.

I have only biographies of Luther's life to reference from. And by no means have I come close to even doing a good college level report on the man, but indulge me if you will while I hypothesis a bit and try to look into the man himself.

If we take what we know to be true, and add some reasonable conjecture, I picture Luther as a restless man. In the early part of his "career," he lectured on the Psalms, the books of Hebrews, Romans, and Galatians. Books filled with God's grace and mercy, where the price of admission into God's kingdom was significantly different then the price the church of the day was giving to the masses.

As he (Luther) studied from those books of the Bible, he became convinced that the church was corrupt in how it defined righteousness. Particularly in the area of penance and the selling of indulgences to gain favor with God. He saw a church that was using the ignorance of its flock to support a lavish life style; one that had lost sight of some of the central truths of Christianity, the most important, of which for Luther, was the doctrine of justification. The doctrine of justification of course being declared righteous by God through *faith* in God's *grace* alone. He then began to teach that salvation or redemption is a gift of God's grace, attainable only through faith in Jesus as the Messiah.

Was this a "bolt of lightning" that hit him one morning or evening? A sudden revelation that he and others had it all wrong? I don't know, and I really couldn't find a definitive historical answer to that question so I'm going to surmise that revelation for him comes like it comes for a lot of us; a piece at a time, until suddenly the picture starts to crystallize.

I like watching the wheel of fortune on TV sometimes. It's a game show that has all the words of a phrase turned over and you are just given a general clue as to the subject. As the contestants guess letters, we at home can guess and second guess with them and watch the phrase unfold. I'm not that good at it. Sometimes I get it pretty quickly, sometimes all but a couple of letters are left and I still don't get it. In those cases, when the phrase is finally revealed, I'll invariably respond; "Oh man! I should have got that! That's obvious now that I see it!"

Isn't that true with the word of God often in our life? You might be down a path that seems quite clear, and suddenly, or not so suddenly a restlessness starts to happen within you, and if you're the type of person that examines that rather then ignoring it; well incredible changes sometime time happen.

That's what I imagine with Luther. A brilliant, devoted Monk, studying and teaching the word of God as he had learned it. Sensing and seeing a disconnect that eventually he couldn't ignore. Did it take a day, a month, a year; perhaps more? We don't know, but eventually the call was strong and he did what he *knew* he must do, and the rest is history.

The Roman Catholic theology of the day stated that faith alone, whether fiduciary or dogmatic, cannot justify man; and that only such faith as is active in charity and good works can justify mans natural sinful nature. And of course, these good works could be obtained by donating money to the church!

It was October 31 of 1517 (ever after known as Reformation Day) that Luther nailed his *95 Theses* on the Castle Church of Wittenberg (The church door was the town bulletin board of the day), which eventually led to his excommunication.

This was heresy; at least as far as the Roman Catholic Church was concerned, Luther was a heretic. Eventually, at the Diet of Worms assembly over freedom of conscience in 1521, Luther's confrontation with the Holy Roman Emperor Charles V over what he had written resulted in that excommunication, and him being declared an outlaw of the state.

If that was it, if this would have been the sum total of his contribution to Christianity, he would still be remembered as a remarkable man, but much more was yet to come.

As I mentioned before, his translation of the Bible into a common language changed countless lives, those who now had the gift of God's word that they never other wise would have. In subsequent years he came to recognize that small local churches and parishes had no formal teaching tool to instruct its people in how to read and interpret God's word. His development of catechetical instruction still stands today. And of course his contribution in the area of great hymns of faith has also stood the test of time. In short; truly a man of God.

And yet, like all of us, he had a side to his character that is difficult to fully understand. His anti-Semitism is more than troubling, and from my point of view speaks to some of the flawed logic of the reformed faith. The whole idea of predestination is one that as I get older, I increasingly view as a narrow window of thought. More and more I see all people at a level playing field at the foot of the cross, and from what I've learned; Luther did not.

But his contribution is undeniable. There was a moment in time; perhaps it was fairly short, or it may have taken several years that he came to realize that God had something special for him to do; and he did it! Isn't that the call of man?

Chapter 8

"John Wesley"

"Time"

This thing, all things devours
Birds, beasts, trees and flowers
It knaws iron, rust's steel
And turns hard stone to meal
It slays Kings! It ruins towns!
And brings high mountains down.

by
J.R.R.Tolkien

John Wesley was born in Epworth England, 20 miles or so North of London, in 1703. The 15th Child of Samuel and Susanna, his father was a graduate of the University of Oxford and a Church of England rector. Of the 19 children Samuel and Susanna had, only 7 lived beyond childhood, including John's famous hymn writing brother, Charles.

His first "moment in time" came when he was barley five years old. Rescued from the burning rectory where is father served, the escape made a deep impression on his mind, and he considered himself "providentially" set apart. His parents gave young John his early education and then at age 11 he went to the Charterhouse school in London.

While at the school he was one of those kids that got "picked on." He was tormented by his classmates, and made to do the sordid things that bullies make weaker individuals do. The insight he gained from these incidents was remarkable for a young teenaged boy. In his own words; "They gave me a fear of God, for if mere children do these things, could not also God do worse?"

Wesley late teens and early adulthood were greatly influenced by classic works on faith that he devoured. Thomas Kempis's book *The Imitation of Christ,* an William Law's two books *Christian Perfection* and *A Serious Call to Devout and Holy Life* made a lasting impression. He was ready for his first adult assignment.

In 1735 John and his brother Charles sailed for Savannah, Georgia in the American colonies at the request of Governor James Oglethorpe who wanted Wesley to be the minister of the newly formed Savannah church. On the ocean voyage to the colonies a violent storm hit them and broke of the mast of the ship. A second moment in time occurred for young John. He observed a group of Moravian settlers calmly singing hymns and praying while the English on board panicked. He was deeply influenced by the depth of their faith and spirituality rooted in pietism. They had an inner strength that he lacked, and he desperately wanted it as well. The personal relationship with Christ that he saw played out in the Moravians heavily influenced Wesley's theology of Methodism.

The Georgia experience was clouded with a broken love affair and self doubt of his ability to preach and lead. When he returned to England in 1738 he was exhausted and struggled with self doubt. He needed the hand of God to restore his confidence, but he would have to take a critical first step.

<>

I'm going to take a quick departure from his biography to make an observation. Here was John at a crossroads in his life. he came back from the colonies bitter, disillusioned, and racked with self doubt. It would have been easy for him perhaps to make a soft choice; perhaps leave the ministry, whatever. And we probably would have never heard about John Wesley again. But he made a different choice, and the rest as we like to say, is history.

He returned to England and heard a reading of Martin Luther's preface to the Epistle of Romans by the Apostle Paul. It was May the 24th, 1738 at a Moravian meeting in Alders gate Street, London. It so impressed Wesley that he penned his now famous lines of *"I felt my heart strangely warmed,"* and it revolutionized the character and method of his ministry. A few weeks after this event, Wesley preached a sermon on the doctrine of personal salvation by faith, and shortly after another on God's grace "free in all, and free for all."

It was a landmark moment. It revitalized his spirit and crystallized his thinking and beliefs. And though his understanding of both justification and the assurance varied throughout his life, Wesley never stopped preaching the importance of faith for salvation and the witness of God's Spirit, with the belief that one was indeed, the child of God.

His close friend from Oxford, the evangelist George Whitefield, himself and his brother Charles, soon found themselves preaching the Gospel where ever they could to a nation starving for the gift of redemption and grace. You have to remember this was all a pretty radical concept back in those days; the idea of predestination was quite ingrained in the populace, and so many people felt that there was no hope for them. At the time he was still attached to the Moravians, but he started to object to a practice they established called "quietism," so without any previous plan, he created the Methodist Society in England. This of course was the beginning of the Methodist Church that claims 70 million adherents in the world today. That certainly speaks of influence!

From that point (about 1740) on, Wesley and the Methodists were persecuted by clergymen and magistrates because they preached without being ordained or licensed by the Anglican Church. They were perceived as a social threat that disregarded institutions. So the formal church was attacking them, which drove them to the fields and back alleys to preach to the neglected and needy. Wesley felt that the church failed to call sinners to repentance, many clergymen were corrupt, and that people were perishing in their sins. *He believed that he was commissioned by God to bring revival in the church, and no opposition, persecution, or any other obstacles could prevail on the divine urgency and authority of this commission.*

Over time Wesley honed is understanding of God and his redemptive plan into a four part theology that the 20th century Wesley Scholar Albert Outler would define as the Wesleyan Quadrilateral. The core of that theology was "Solo Scriptura" meaning that the living core of Christian faith was revealed in scripture, and that the Bible was the sole foundational source of theological or doctrinal development. The other three parts were, tradition, experience (by the body of believers – not just an individual), and reason. But the three must always be supported by the first: the Bible.

As his ministry grew, so did his responsibilities to it. He ordained laymen as ministers, and setup districts and parishes all over England and Scotland. He was a tireless worker, who often preached three sermons a day, and rode over 250,000 miles by horseback during his long life spreading the gospel. His one unhappy marriage at age 48 to a widow ended 15 years later when she left him, with no children, and he never married again.

When he died at age 88, he left behind a good library, about 140 published sermons, several books of poetry and song, several books dealing on various religious thought, a couple of short Biblical study guides, and the Methodist Church. As a man opposed to slavery, he wrote a pamphlet on the subject in 1774 that was widely read and helped inspire men that would follow him to abolish the English slave trade, most notably Wilbur Wilberforce.

So here again is a man that faced crossroads and choices like we all do. Here is a man that is influenced by events and seemingly random happenings. When they occurred, at that moment in time, he or no one else around him could have even in their wildest imagination predicted the results of the choices being made. But God sees it all, and he in his infinite wisdom laid opportunities at the feet of a man named John Wesley, who walked through the door of faith and changed the world. I believe it with my whole being. It all happened in time.

Chapter 9

"Chuck Colson"

There is a time for everything,
And a season for every activity under heaven:
A time to be born, and a time to die,
A time to plant, and a time to harvest,
A time to kill, and a time to heal,
A time to tear down, and a time to build,
A time to weep, and a time to laugh,
A time to mourn, and a time to dance,
A time to scatter stones, and a time to gather them,
A time to embrace, and a time to refrain,
A time to search, and a time to give up,
A time to keep, and a time to give away,
A time to tear, and a time to mend,
A time to be silent, and a time to speak,
A time to love, and a time to hate,
A time for war, and a time for peace.

I thought in my heart:

"God will bring to judgment,
To both the righteous and the wicked,
For there will be a time for every activity,
A time for every deed.

Ecclesiastes 3: 1-8, 17

Charles Colson of course was a special counselor to Richard Nixon the 37th President of the United States. In his book "Born Again," he details the chain of events that lead to his accepting Jesus Christ as his Savior and Lord. The actual moment of acceptance was very clearly defined for him; what's interesting is the chain of events that lead up to that "moment in time."

As you read his book, you discover that he is a very unhappy man. Here is a guy that was an overachiever all of his life, but when he got to a point where he couldn't think or work his way out of a problem (Watergate), he felt absolutely lost and helpless. Isn't that true for all of us?

God has a way of picking up on our signals when we are floundering; and if we have a heart to hear he provides people and events to help us to come to him. Sometimes slowly, sometimes quickly, but he does provide. And in Colson's case, this was true as well.

In 1973 a few weeks after returning to his private law practice, but before his trial with Watergate, Chuck met an old friend and business associate, a company president for a large manufacturing firm in the northeast.

After normal chit-chat and such, Colson writes in his book that he sensed "something different" about his friend Tom, and it wasn't long before Tom revealed what that difference was.

Chuck asked him a leading question (something to the effect that he had heard that Tom was involved in some "religious activities") and his friend Tom replied; "Yes that's true Chuck. I have accepted Jesus Christ. I have committed my life to him, and it is the most marvelous experience of my life."

Tom went on to tell Chuck about the difference Christ was making in his life, how Christ had rescued him from an empty life and the story effectively shell-shocked Colson. Chuck quickly brought the subject to a more neutral ground, but the die was set. He couldn't get the picture out of his mind of what a change he saw in Tom.

Time passed and Colson went back to the treadmill he was on as the whole Watergate scandal started to heat up around him. As the long hot summer of 1973 progressed Colson increasingly felt more lost and alone in a sea of politics and corruption. Then came a night to remember: on a Sunday night, August the 12th of 1973, Colson arranged another visit with Tom and his life changed.

After small talk, the subject got turned to the place they probably both intuitively knew it would; the large hole in Chuck's life, and his struggle to understand why he was feeling that way.

Tom shared about how he had come to realize his need for a savior; the emptiness of making another sale, closing the deal, influencing people, the homes and cars and stuff that seemed to spell happiness. How futile it all seemed to be after a while.

"It may be hard to understand, Tom said, but I didn't seem to have anything that mattered. It was all on the surface. All the material things in life are worthless if a man hasn't discovered what's underneath them."

Tom talked about how one night when he was in New York City on business he noticed that Billy Graham was having a crusade and on impulse he went to it. And somehow, this time the words of the speaker seemed to all make sense; he was drawn to the message and decided that night to give his life to Christ, and he asked him to be Lord of his life.

So Colson asked; "Is that what you mean by accepting Christ? You just ask?"

"That's it, as simple as that, Tom replied. Of course, you have to want Jesus in your life, really *want* him. That's the way it starts. And let me tell you, and then things began to change. Since then I found a satisfaction and joy about living that I never knew was possible."

Well Chuck had trouble digesting all of that at once. It was really too simple for a man that was used to big and complex problems, so the conversation drifted over to the trouble brewing in Washington and the mess of Watergate.

After some time on that subject, Tom pointed out to Chuck that he wouldn't have found himself in the spot he was in if he had relied on God instead of himself and others; and then he said, "Chuck, I don't think you will understand what I'm saying about God, until you are willing to face yourself honestly and squarely. This is the first step."

And then he started to hand Colson a copy of *"Mere Christianity"* by C.S. Lewis. But before he did, he paused. "Let me read you one chapter."

And so Chuck sat back while the word of C.S. Lewis spilled into the night; Tom had selected the chapter that talked about pride and the words knifed into Colson like none had ever done before. One phrase from the book in particular haunted him; "For pride is a spiritual cancer: it eats up the very possibility of love, or contentment, or even common sense."

It seemed to sum up all of what had been wrong in the White House for the last few years; and it stung as only the truth can.

Tom asked the question. "How about it Chuck?" It jarred Colson into a response; "I've got to be certain. I've got to learn a lot more, be sure all my reservations are satisfied. I've got a lot of intellectual hang-ups to get past."

The moment passed but Tom again took the initiative to ask Chuck if he could pray for him before he left. As he did, Chuck recounts how a warm glow came over him; a wave of energy; then the moment passed.

Chuck's words; "When I left the house the iron grip I had kept on my emotions began to relax and all of a sudden I found myself weeping uncontrollably. I forgot about machismo, about pretenses, about fears of being weak. And then I prayed my first real prayer; "God I don't know how to find you, but I'm going to try! I'm not much the way I am now, but somehow I want to give myself to you.""

What a defining moment! Was Charles Colson's quest over just because of that night? Hardly. He would go on to face some of the greatest challenges of his life; *which often happens when we make a decision to turn our life and our will over to God;* but it was a watershed moment. A place he could look back to and say; "this was the moment I could not turn back from, nothing else will ever be quite the same."

And it wasn't. Colson went on to face the Watergate trial, and he along with others were actually imprisoned for their part in the cover-up. But as that was all unfolding in his life, he began to earnestly seek God, and what was true for him is true for all of us; when you seek him, he reveals himself to you.

Colson went on to become a celebrated Christian Author, a man that started an incredible prison ministry, and certainly a man that has helped change countless lives. There was a moment in time where he could have gone either way; if his friend Tom had not quietly persisted, if C.S. Lewis had never written his book, you get it. The chain of events that can only be described as miracles when you look back on them; just moments in time.

Chapter 10

"C.S. Lewis"

Now, Today, This moment,
Is our chance to choose the right side.
God is holding back to give us that chance.
It will not last forever.
We must take it or leave it.

by
C.S. Lewis
" Mere Christianity"

I really enjoy reading C.S. Lewis. One of the primary reasons is because he has a unique way of making his point and validating his hypothesis. He has a way of making a circular argument for his thesis that doesn't leave room for off and on ramps. Born in Belfast Ireland on November 29, 1898, he was raised in the church, but he became an atheist at age 15. A brilliant student, he went on to Oxford, where he became a companion of J.R.R. Tolkien the famed author of The *Hobbit & the Lord of the Rings* Trilogy. Partially through Tolkien's influence and also the book *The Everlasting Man* by G.K. Chesterton, Lewis slowly rediscovered Christianity.

Lewis spoke of his conversion; "You must picture me alone; night after night, feeling, whenever my mind lifted even a second from my work, the steady, unrelenting approach of him whom I so earnestly desired not to meet. That which I feared had at last come upon me, in the Trinity term of 1929 I gave in, and admitted God was God, and I knelt and prayed. Perhaps, that night, the most dejected and reluctant convert in all of England."

Wow! What a confession! Can you relate? I can! Why the dejection and reluctance? Because Lewis knew, as well did I, that when we make a decision to follow Christ and have him live in us, nothing is ever the same. We need to "die to self." That's a process that takes a lifetime, and is never completely over.

So somewhere in the process of turning our life over to Christ, we need to also understand what is right and wrong; don't we? Lewis makes some observations: "It's not our job to blame people when they behave badly, but we do need to know if the behavior they are displaying is good or bad. And we can only do that if we have somewhat of an understanding of the difference between right and wrong. For instance, a man occupying the seat at the diner I want and the man that took my seat when my back was turned are both equally inconvenient; but I blame the one and not the other. Just like every note and key on the piano can be either a right note or a wrong note; it depends upon when it is played."

So the truth is that we need help defining what is right and wrong. Man in and of himself is incapable of doing that; and Lewis with his keen intellect weaves an extraordinary circular argument in his book *"Mere Christianity"* that illustrates that point and makes it one of the foundation blocks for his presentation of the authenticity of Christ, *and* the message of salvation he brings through God's holy word.

Due to Lewis's approach to religious belief as a skeptic, and his following conversion, he has been called "The Apostle to the Skeptics."

In a much cited passage from *"Mere Christianity,"* Lewis challenged the increasingly popular view that Jesus, although a great moral teacher, was not God. He argued that Jesus made several implicit claims to divinity, which would logically exclude this possibility. He writes:

"I am trying here to prevent anyone saying the really foolish thing that people often say about Him: 'I'm ready to accept Jesus as a great moral teacher, but I don't accept his claim as God.' That is one thing we must not say. A man who is merely a man and said the sort of things that Jesus said would not be a great moral teacher. He would either be a lunatic – on a level with the man who says he is a poached egg – or else he would be the Devil of Hell. You must make your choice. Either this man was, and is, the Son of God, or else a madman or something worse. You can shut him up for being a fool, you can spit at him, and kill him as a demon, or you can fall at his feet and call him Lord and God, but let us not come with any patronizing nonsense about his being a great human teacher. He did not leave that open to us. He did not intend to."

This is an argument, sometimes referred to as "Lewis's trilemma," although he did not invent it, he did develop and popularize it. It has also been used by the Christian apologist Josh McDowell in his book; *More Than a Carpenter.*

One of Lewis's main thesis in his apologia, is that there is a common morality known throughout humanity. In his first five chapters of *Mere Christianity*, Lewis discusses the idea that people have a standard of behavior to which they expect other people to adhere. He defines this as a Universal Morality, or Natural Law. He writes:

"These then are the two points that I wanted to make. First, that human beings, all over the earth, have this curious idea that they ought to behave in a certain way, and cannot really get rid of it. Secondly, that they do not in fact behave that way. They know the law of nature; they break it. These two facts are the clear foundation of all clear thinking about ourselves and the universe we live in."

Really, Lewis is just paraphrasing the Apostle Paul from Romans 7 where Paul talks about doing the evil he wishes not to do. But the point is made. Lewis does an excellent job throughout his writing of pointing out mans sinful nature, the fact that he recognizes it, and is powerless to control it in his own free will.

And so all through Lewis's writing, his works of fiction and of non-fiction, he again and again illustrates this classic struggle of man. Good versus Evil. Right against wrong. Free will, and submission to the will of God. And he does a wonderful job of helping us understand our part, and God's part. We both have a role in our salvation!

I read Lewis as a young boy, a young man, and again in recent years as I've tried to hone my understanding of who I am and what my beliefs and values are. I'm not suggesting that Lewis has all the answers, and that you will be less complete as an individual if his thoughts and writings aren't integrated into your way of life. I am suggesting however that here is a man, that at "a moment in time," quite actually a number of different moments in time, realized that he could not live life the same if he chose to believe in Christ. And so for him, the course of his life started to unfold in a different direction since that point. As an educator, and author, and a speaker, that conversion dramatically altered his path. And it opened up doors and windows of opportunity that he could never have imagined before. And he did influence people. Many people, over many years, in many places. And he has influenced me. And perhaps I may influence you. Time will tell, and God will know.

C.S. Lewis was given a number of gifts. A brilliant mind. The influence and opportunity to engage with others, that also had brilliant minds. Education and opportunity. He also received that vexing still small voice that over time he could not ignore. Thank-you, for not ignoring those thoughts, oh so long ago on that Trinity Trimester night when you felt the call of God and knew a decision had to be made. The world will never be the same. *I* will never be the same. It all happened in a moment of time.

Chapter 11

"Brad"

"The Future is something which everyone reaches at the same rate of sixty minutes an hour, whatever he does, whoever he is."

by
C.S. Lewis

Do you remember the first time you heard about Jesus? Brad can still remember it today. He recalls; "I was at my Aunts house, I was four or five years old, and we were having vacation Bible school in a neighbor's backyard when my teacher told me; "If you ask for it, he (Jesus) will give it to you." So I asked, If I pray for a go-cart will I get it?" When the teacher explained that Jesus may not give him a go-cart, but he will always give you want you need, the young Brad was satisfied; but it would take years for him to discern the difference between need and want. As is true for most of us.

Brad is a glass "all the way" full kind of guy. He also happens to be my boss. Likeable, intelligent, hard working; he is the type of man that others will naturally fall behind. A born salesman, he could not only sell igloos to Eskimos, he could also sell them to residents of countries at the equator! When he makes a presentation of the wall panel system he invented and developed, your convinced of the quality and ease of application; the first time you hear him. In addition, he's a guy that tells the truth; and he knows how to admit his own mistakes, and the mistakes of his company. His insistence that "we always do the next right thing" is probably the main reason we are having the success we are today; not to mention the fact that we really do have a great product to offer the consumer.

He's a devoted husband, father, a strong believer, and a great boss. He also knows today that God's not finished with him yet. How does, how did, he get from being that wide eyed boy to where he is? Like all of us; there's a story.

His parents divorced at the age of 12 and Brad felt a strong sense of responsibility to be the "man" of the family. He developed a strong protective instinct to his younger brother that is still in his DNA today. He had a great, quality relationship with his Grandfather on his mother's side that he still remembers with great fondness. "He took me under his wing, and made me feel important. Brad told me, He was very affirming, and helped me to believe in myself; he took me to church, and his influence helped to solidify my belief in Jesus."

Brad was one of those kids that always had a sense of purpose. He wanted to work and have success and live the "good" life, and like so many of us, got caught in the trap of materialisim that was hard for him to escape. "One of the things I did right, Brad shared, was finding his wife Diane. I was still in High School. He recalled; I saw her from across the room, I didn't even know her name, and said; "she's the one." I immediately broke up with the girl I was dating, and went home and told Mom that I found the girl that I was going to marry. Continuing with his story, Brad said; "Now all I had to do was find out who she was, and let her in on the secret!"

Diane and Brad, true to his prediction, got married at age 18 and have never looked back. "From an earthly perspective, she has been the best thing that ever could have happened to me. Brad said; I'm more in love with her every day."

What drives certain people to "do whatever it takes" to succeed, while others burn and fizzle, or never even ignite at all? Over lunch, Brad and I reflected on that, and both shared with each other some of our personal experiences. I was struck with the underlying intensity that is part of Brad's personality as he told me more about his business up and downs.

He has worked in the construction industry all of his life, with his initial focus being on the glass and curtain wall industry. This led to an interest in different types of siding options and he began to discover a potential for building a business that would specialize in that area. His first major foray into the panel field included a very cool, unique, product that was developed in France. Brad poured his heart into the opportunity, and soon he had the groundwork in-place for an extremely successful national program; of which he was the sole distributer. Just less than a year later, the product started to fail in the field because of design flaws, and Brad was forced to shut down the operation.

Faced with pending bankruptcy and the failure of his business, Brad faced a test so many before him have also had to deal with. Where did I go wrong? What do I do now?

What is it about our human condition that draws us away from a dependence on the Lord? It's the *human condition*! The devil would like nothing better than for us to become un-dependant on God. And he does that subtly; attacking us at our point of weakness.

Brad was given an extraordinary gift of being able to make things happen, and he channeled that gift into business; and had success. But when things went south as things will do; he found himself on his knees acknowledging his shortcomings and his inability to manage the problem in his own strength.

When we start to put our dependence on God, things start to happen. It may not be what we *think* we want to have happen, but happen it does. God gave Brad the strength of character to "do the next right thing." He refused bankruptcy and created a plan to pay back all of his debts; in full. It would take years; but he did it. God also gave Brad the resiliency to not give up. During all of this time he downsized his business but held it together. Sometimes with smoke and mirrors, but it held together. It was during that time frame he continued to develop exterior panel ideas and actually invented a system that he was able to get patents on, and begin to market.

Do you see the various moments in time in his life that God was asking Brad to depend on him? To turn his will over? Again, Brad got tested when it became apparent his new product and company were going to need partners in order to get up and running. Brad prayed for God's hand in all of it, but he admitted to me that he still wanted control. "Tom, it wasn't until I said to God ; "OK, not my will but your will be done," that God started opening the doors for me to move forward. I hope it's a lesson I don't ever forget."

Today, our company with Brad at its helm is doing remarkable in a very difficult economy. Our mantra, which Brad infuses into the organization is "Do the right thing." We have a dedicated team of people that work hard to do just that. And we have a guy at the top that is cognizant of where his blessing and strength have come from.

We talked about all of this over lunch, and we both recognize our human condition that will quickly make us believe that it is our hard work and cleverness that gives us these blessings. This is just another story of how God works in our lives; when we let him. The exciting news is that there is more to be revealed! There is a whole group of people (family, employees, associates) that can attest to that.

As God continues to work in Brad's life, the influence potential continues to grow. As we are faithful with the little things, new opportunities for his kingdom work get revealed. We again get to see that played out in an individuals life; this time it's Brad, tomorrow it will be someone else, a moment at a time.

Chapter 12

"John Haggia"

"Moment by moment I'm kept in his love;
Moment by moment I've life from above.
Looking to Jesus till glory doth shine,
Moment by moment, O Lord, I am thine."

by
D.W. Whittle
1893

Born in Louisville Kentucky in the early part of the 20th Century, John is still an active teacher, preacher, author, and the head of his own institute for developing Christian leaders, as he lives in his ninth decade.

John first came to my attention at a pivotal moment in my own life. It was the summer of 1988 and my personal world was in a state of turmoil.

Struggling with my addiction to alcohol and my personal identity were just a couple of the things going on in my life that floundering summer. Bigger still was my sense of being really lost spiritually, although I don't think I had actually identified that at the time. Regardless, a door of opportunity opened for me one day and I chose to step through it. On the other side of that door was John Haggai and what happened the next two days are just as fresh as if they happened yesterday.

<>

He had been invited into town on a Saturday to give a one day leadership seminar to local area businessmen, and then he was slated to be the guest speaker the following morning at Central Wesleyan Church of Holland. I was given an invitation to attend the workshop in which he went through 12 principles of Christian Leadership that he had outlined in his new book *"Lead On!"* He gave every participant a copy of the book, and his message that day inspired me to take a closer look at my walk with God.

The following day, I made it a point to go to Central Wesleyan to here him preach. It was the first time I had ever been in the church and for the first time in my life I really felt the spirit of the Lord washing over me as we worshiped and sang that day. It inspired me to continue going there which ultimately led me to a closer walk with Jesus, and even though I have had a lot of rough day's in my life since then, I still consider it a "moment in time" for me that has helped make me who I am today. So the Lords calling on John's life has special meaning for me.

John's father was a clergyman, and Christianity and faith were a part of who John was and is from very early childhood. A gifted student and a hardworking young man, John excelled in the class room and was a recognized leader when he graduated from the Moody Bible Institute in 1945.

Over the next twenty-plus years as he honed his skills and sharpened his vision, a path became clear to him of which direction his life should go. At age six he already knew he wanted to be a preacher. By age ten he already sensed that his life would be involved with world-wide missions. As he grew, he felt a clear and strong calling that he should devote his life to developing Christian leaders that could spread their influence to a world that desperately needed them. But as is true for most of us, he faced a test.

It was 1969. Heavily in debt because of his efforts to get his new ministry off the ground floor, and in addition spending a good deal of his income to care for an invalided son, he was at a crossroads. In pursuit of his God-given vision, he had sunk every available dollar into an ambitious global training venture that even some of his best friends dismissed as folly.

With a severely depleted income, he cashed in insurance policies, decimated his savings; he even sold his car. If he didn't make the next mortgage payment, he would even lose his house.

What occurred next forced him to make one of the toughest decisions he ever had to make. We received a call from Dr. Wendell Philips.

I pick up the story in John's own words from his introduction to his best selling book *"How to Win Over Worry."*

As a young man, Phillips had led a series of daring exploits in the Middle East that would later inspire the Hollywood character Indiana Jones. At the age of 26 he had set off to find the remains of the Queen of Sheba's palace, and ended up in a dramatic showdown with the local Yemeni warlords.

Now, a couple of decades latter, his extensive work in the Middle East had made him the world's largest independent oil concessionaire. He'd heard of my own roots in the Middle East on my father's side. He had a proposal to make.

"I want you to work for me for 12 months, he said. I'll pay you one million dollars upon signing our contract. In addition I'll split the overriding royalty interest with you on any oil discoveries."

By any measurement, this was a fabulous offer. As it turned out, a huge discovery would shortly be made in North Africa, yielding 37 million under the terms of Philip's contract.

But for me, it came at a price.

I sat at my desk and contemplated a future filled with Wendell Philip's money – and a God-given vision that would almost certainly die if I stepped aside at this crucial moment to rescue my finances.

I knew I had no choice.

"I'm sorry, I told him. I can't do it."

He sounded stunned. "What's the matter? He said, is it not enough money?"

"No, I replied. Your job is to small."

Wow. Is my faith that strong? Is my trust in the Lord big enough to stand up to that kind of offer? A moment in time isn't always just about turning your life to Christ. Many times in your walk with Christ you face a moment when perhaps he calls you to greater service and perhaps sacrifice. How do you and I respond?

For John Haggai, it took over twenty two years for him to dig out of the financial hole that he allowed in his life, to pursue the vision he felt led to. Not many men would let a vision come in front of their financial comfort, but he did.

John felt a strong calling on his life at an early age to develop leaders; specifically Christian leaders that would be about the business of spreading the gospel to a world that badly needs it. He had crossroad moments in time that he could have taken an easier, softer way. But he didn't.

He also recognized that one of the primary leadership opportunities that most of us get in life, is right in the home. A call to leadership as a parent has never been more needed than it is right now.

His thoughts on leadership are so good in my opinion, that I've included part of his summary from his book *"Lead On,"* in the next couple of paragraphs.

John writes: *"What is leadership? It is the discipline of deliberately exerting special influence within a group to move it toward goals of beneficial permanence that fulfill the real needs of the group. Leaders are made, not born. Admittedly, some people have more aptitude for leadership than others, but if a person has a burning desire to lead, they can attain leadership success."*

That says a lot, doesn't it? Here is a man that worked hard to understand what effective leadership looked like, and how critical it was to train people in this discipline correctly, so that he could achieve the vision he felt given to him by God for world wide evangelism.

So where does that vision stand today? As of early 2010, over 77,500 men and women have graduated from the Haggai Institute since 1969, serving in over 183 counties. Thousands more are on the waiting list to be taught. The lives changed for Christ are hard to quantify, but it is safe to say that the work of the institute has had a profound impact on world evangelism.

Crossroads. Decisions. Moments in time. We all have them, John had and still has his, and the world will never be the same.

Chapter 13

"Scott"

"Carpe diem quam minimum credula postero"

Seize the day, and put no trust in the future

Author Unknown

The caveat to that statement might be: don't put your trust in earthly things. Certainly, we trust and believe in a future with our heavenly father. As does Scott. But not at first. Not by a long shot.

Born July 20, 1972 in Cassopolis Michigan, Scott lived with his Mom, Dad, and younger brother in a nice home on a lake just outside of town. His dad was a foreman for an electric company, and his mom was a nurse, so there was plenty of money, and a sense of normalcy and lack of worry when Scott was a young boy growing up.

There wasn't any spiritual guidance or regular church attendance for young Scott, other than a neighbor who would somewhat frequently take him and his younger brother Matt to the local church. For Scott, it was a social function only that had no spiritual impact that he could discern then, or now.

When Scott was about 12 or 13 years old, he woke up one morning to find his Dad packing dishes into boxes. He asked his Dad what was going on and was told that he and his Mother were getting a Divorce. It was the first clue that Scott had ever had that there was something wrong in the marriage. What does a kid of thirteen do? Offered the opportunity to either stay with his mother and younger brother, or move with his dad to Texas; he decided on Texas.

Up to this point, Scott's life had been pretty normal. True, he and a buddy raided the liquor cabinet one afternoon and got really drunk; but he was just your average young teenager.

When Scott and his dad went to Texas, things changed. First of all, Scotts dad had Huntington's disease and was on disability by this point in his life. Secondly, once they got down to Texas (San Antonio) the house that they rented became like a frat house. Scott's dad started buying him beer. Women came and went out of the house. Within a few short months Scott's life had gone from a pretty normal teenager to a dysfunctional relationship with his dad and a quickly developing party habit.

After about four months of this, they got homesick, packed everything up, and moved back to southern Michigan. Dad bought a trailer, and a cycle of shuffling between parents, increasing drug and alcohol use, and deteriorating performances in school and at home, were becoming the norm.

By now Scott is 17, has a pregnant girlfriend, has dropped out of school, and has a full blown drug and alcohol problem. A cycle of rehab's, getting clean and then falling off the wagon were becoming routine. The girlfriend had the baby, and Scott went from work, to out of control drug and alcohol use, to rehab's. It didn't take long before the girlfriend and Scott's baby were gone. He was a hard worker when sober and started to learn a trade as a mason, but it was certainly not a tame lifestyle. God was a million miles away.

Scott was 19 years old when he met Kenlynn his future wife through a mutual friend. An instant attraction between the two was the beginning of a long road ahead for the young couple. His lifestyle of "me first" was very well ingrained so as you can imagine the relationship had unhealthy dynamics at the beginning. And Kenlynn shared in some of the lifestyle choices by drinking and partying with Scott to a point. But Scott's train ride to nowhere was just starting to build up steam; it would take a wreck or a miracle to stop it.

It was about this time that his dad took his own life. Very ill from his Huntington's disease, he bought a shotgun, took it back to his house, and ended his life with a single shot to the head. Scott, who was living with a friend at the time got a phone call from his mother that no had had heard from his dad for a few days, and maybe Scott should go check on him. Doing just that, Scott found him dead on the couch, the TV still on, his life over.

The depths of depravity that the evil one (Satan) will drive us to, reared its ugly head for Scott that evening. After calling 911, he went back over to his dad's body and stole his cash and some checks. Even in a moment like that the grip of addiction and sin can be so powerful that we will do anything to feed it.

The next couple of years were a blur for Scott. The drug and alcohol use continued to escalate, but he did get married to Kenlynn when he was 22 and they quickly had two children. They moved to Long Island New York, were the cycle of working hard, going on binges, coming back and straightening up for a week or two, became an all to familiar pattern.

After a vacation back to Michigan a couple of years into their marriage, they decided to move back to Cassopolis. Nothing changed about their life, other than the location. Living in a rent free modular home proved by Kenlynn's grandparents, Scott barely provided the necessary provisions for his young family.

Kenlynn was and is a remarkable woman. A Christian who was frustrated and hurt by her husband's choices, she also felt a strong calling to "stand by her man." Everyone knew about Scott's lifestyle and Kenlynn confided in her grandparents and they in turn confided in a couple of pastors from the local church. They came to visit Scott after his binge's and received nothing but empty words in return; anything to make them go away.

It's now late July of 1999. Kenlynn has had enough and tells Scott he needs to leave. Scott does and goes on a horrific two week binge. When he gets back he tells Kenlynn that he needs to go into the hospital. Scott is 27 years old, his body is beat up, his marriage is in shambles, he has been in six in-patient rehabs, and God is nowhere to be found. Or is he?

After some initial drama where he ripped the IV's out his arm and tried to run away, the hospital got him settled and made arrangements to have him transferred to a State Hospital. At the last minute an opening became available at the Chester Ray treatment house in Holland Michigan, and Scott was sent there instead. Timing can be everything.

Chester Ray is a male in-patient treatment center for guys suffering from drug and alcohol addictions sponsored by OAR, the parent clinic. Scott arrived with a bag of clothes and four days of sobriety. That was all he had in the world. It was August 17, 1999.

The Chester Ray house has been in Holland for almost 40 years. At any given moment it houses up to 14 different guys, plus in-house staff. Guys come there in all shapes and sizes, with one common thread. Their life has become unmanageable. For those who have never experienced that totally lost feeling, it's hard to explain. Like a test pilot that has tried everything he knows of to get his plane out of its deathly tailspin, the desert floor is looming quickly, and he better hit his eject switch; or die.

There are rules that need to be followed. You get up at a certain time. You eat, do chores, exercise, have class, and go to meetings as a group. There is one-on-one time with counselors, opportunities to develop meaningful relationships, and a core value of affirmation and having Christ at the center of your recovery. If you have the gift of desperation and a willingness to receive. Many do not and fail. Scott did and was ready.

Sometimes you meet an individual when you are at the point of readiness that is so instrumental in your recovery, that when you look back on it with the perspective of time and distance, you see God's hand all through it. Mr. Al was such a man in Scott's life. Over the next 100 days Scott got serious about recovery. He was sick and tired of being sick and tired. He recognized his inability to manage his own life. He came to believe a power greater than himself could restore his life to sanity. He became willing to surrender his will to the care of God, and he asked Christ to come in his life. Al helped Scott with a multitude of questions. He helped teach him how to pray. He showed Scott how he could be set free from the bondage of sin. He helped save Scott's life.

Other things began to happen as well. Scott started attending NA (Narcotics Anonymous) meetings on a regular basis. He started to develop relationships with individuals within the program that had something that he wanted. A quality drug free life that had meaning and purpose. He and Kenlynn started going to a local church together and began putting the past behind, and started building on the here and now. And he was diligent about working the steps of the program of recovery, not perfectly, but he stayed clean and sober one day at a time, and kept going to meetings. He was on the road.

It was shortly after he got out of Chester Ray and he and Kenlynn were renting a house when a local builder stopped by. A strong Christian, Jerry had heard about Scott through a friend of a friend and went to Scott to ask him if he wanted to have a job. Scott agreed, and within a month he had become so valuable that he earned a company truck and was starting to take the lead on projects. Can you see the hand of God when we choose to do our part?

<>

Fast forward with me to the present. Scott and Kenlynn have 6 children (5 boys and a baby girl), a nice home, Scott has a good job, and he recently celebrated 10 years of sobriety and clean time from drugs. He is leading his family. He has brought other individuals to Christ through his witness in NA. He has sponsored recovering addicts and has helped change lives within that community. He is currently planning his second trip to Slovakia to help spread the good news of Christ centered recovery. He has volunteered his time and skills to fix up peoples properties when they couldn't. He has served on NA's local advisory board. He has given time to distribute food to the needy through a local ministry. And he has become one of my very good friends.

What is a friend? It is a person that brings multiple dimensions and gifts to a relationship. They are caring, good listeners, encouragers, people you can just have fun with. They are accepting, willing to sacrifice for the sake of the friendship, they recognize need without being told. They help you think more clearly, they educate, they challenge, and they love intentionally. They model Christ in their lives; not perfectly, but they keep trying.

Scott is such a friend to me, and also many others. He had a moment in his life when he realized that he needed to turn his will over to God if he was going to stand a chance at truly living. He chose to do that, and his family, friends, and community are the grateful recipient. For Scott there have been pivotal moments of time; and there will be more in his future. How he, how we, respond is everything; at that special, crucial, moment in time.

Chapter 14

"Henri Nouwen"

"Me thinks I see the wanton hours flee,
And as they pass, turn back and laugh at me."

by
George Villiers

Henri Joseph Machiel Nouwen was a Dutch-born Catholic priest and writer who authored over 40 books in his lifetime.

Of the many works he authored, I have read only a few, but those books have deeply impacted my own spiritual journey. Books such as *"The Return of the Prodigal Son, & The Life of the Beloved,"* are two of his outstanding works on the unconditional love that our father God has for us. With incredible insight, he weaves a masterful story in *"The Return of the Prodigal Son,"* that illustrates that love not only from the son's perspective, but from the elder brother's and his father as well.

Although describing love and forgiveness as unconditional is not a novel idea, or a novel thing to write about, they way he wove the story in *"The Return of the Prodigal Son,"* is so singular, at least in my experience, that is worth repeating here. With the lost younger son, he describes and shows a life of the beloved (himself) that is full of misery because he thinks he can only be loved by meeting certain qualifications of the lover (his father). The elder son's actions, or lack thereof, shows how the beloved can be depressed because he thinks he deserves greater love because he has done all the right things. The father alone knows how to love, forgive, and give proper leadership, while still being happy and content in all things.

I have been all of those in my life; and as I strive to fit into a father's role with my children, and try to understand how to be a son to my father without the dysfunction, I way to often find my self living as the younger or elder son in the story.

Henri Nouwen lived a life that always had a pretty clearly defined direction. As a young boy, he already felt drawn into the priesthood. In fact, when he was just eight years old he converted his parents attic into a children's chapel. Certainly, not the things I was doing or thinking at age eight.

Although he grew up in the Netherlands, he was schooled in the United States. While in the seminary, he developed an interest in psychology and in 1964 was named a fellow in the program for religion and psychiatry at the Menninger Foundation in Topeka, Kansas. After which, he joined the faculty at Notre Dame University.

Here is an individual that always felt from an early age that he was to be an ambassador for God. So there isn't that sharply defined moment in time that his world changed. And there also is not that long period of time where values changed subtly. What there is with him is a picture of a man who was always restless trying to understand himself, how he was wired, and what God's mission for him looked like.

He suffered from depression a good deal of his adult life. He struggled with his sexuality. He had a consuming need for affection, intimacy, and friendship. He had a network of friends around the world and often would call them in the middle of the night and keep them up for hours because of his need for companionship at that particular moment.

Nouwen was a mystic in the sense that he was deeply spiritual. He was a priest who tried to follow the mystical path through earnest prayer and a disciplined life focused on the Eucharist. He read scripture carefully, studied many of the spiritual classics, and was drawn to God through icons and other forms of art. Even though he tried very hard to have a fully developed prayer life, he struggled in this area, and as a point of fact, his deepest contemplative thoughts often happened when he was writing; these were the times of solitude and centering for him.

As I write about Nouwen, I am struck by the fact that he had multiple moments of time in his life where he journeyed from a place of comfort and peace with his God, and to places were he felt tortured, and lost, so very alone. He is a man who seems to have experienced those highs and lows at greater levels of intensity then perhaps you and I. And his work reflects that.

Carolyn Whitney-Brown always believed there was more to Henri then whatever got into his books. She wrote: *" His vision of what was possible and his horizons were always bigger than his ability to live them out."* I believe that may be true for all of us.

Henri had a number of watershed moments in his life. His ability to communicate to Christians of various denominations with broad appeal made him a much sought after speaker and lecturer in the prime of his life. In a 1994 survey of 3,400 U.S. Protestant church leaders, he was named as their second greatest influence, ahead of Billy

Graham. He appealed to Evangelicals because he honored the historic essence of the Christian faith, and was never into revisionism.

Many site Nouwen's book *"The Wounded Healer"* as his greatest contribution to society at large. Certainly the primary thesis that he communicates in this work is actually one that he repeats over and over again in his many other literary efforts. In fact, some people point out that if you have read one of Nouwen's books, you've read them all. I don't quite agree with that, but the point is made: his thoughts on the human condition of loneliness and abandonment are central themes in much of what he writes.

In *"The Wounded Healer"* he writes about that void: *We ignore what we know with a deep-seated intuitive knowledge. That no love or friendship, no intimate embrace or tender kiss, no community, commune or collective, no man or woman, will ever be able to satisfy our desire to be released from our lonely condition. This truth is so disconcerting and painful that we are more prone to play games with our fantasies than to face the truth of our existence. Thus we keep hoping that one day we will find the man who really understands our experiences, the woman who will bring peace to our restless life, the job where we can fulfill our potentials, the book that will explain everything, and the place where we can feel at home. Such false hope leads us to make exhausting demands and prepares us for bitterness and dangerous hostility when we discover that nobody, and nothing, can live up to our absolutistic expectations."*

Of course the answer is that no human being, or man made thing, can ever satisfy the void in our spirit apart from Christ. And Nouwen knew that, preached it, wrote about it, taught it, yet struggled as much as any man with accepting God's unconditional grace in his own life.

I've included Nouwen in this book because he has influenced myself and many others with his work. I doesn't have the sharply defined moment of time that many others have had that I've written about. God was part of his conscience from an early age. But he is like so many of us from the standpoint that he personally found less peace for himself, then the gift of peace and reconciliation he was able to minister to others.

It's a good lesson for me. And hopefully for you as well. Not to allow the evil one to rob us of the gift God so freely provides if we but fully trust him. The gift of peace. I'm grateful for Henri's gift of helping make that clear.

Chapter 15

"Justin"

"Time, a cradle of hope: wisdom walks before it, opportunity with it, and repentance behind it. He that has made it his friend will have little to fear from his enemies, but he that has made it his enemy will have little to hope from his friends."

by
Charles Colton

On Thursday, February 19 2009, I met with my good friends Ken, Dan, Ken's wife Jean, a few other men, and Justin and his wife Sue. I went there for the express purpose of supporting Justin as he rededicated his life to Christ, and chose that time, and the place we were at, to draw a line in the sand and say; "This is it. I commit before God and these witnesses that I am making a deliberate paradigm change, to live my life differently." Surely this, is a moment in time.

Justin's fist moment in time came on June 11, 1973. The oldest of 4 children born into their family, he lived an unremarkable childhood and adolescence by worldly standards, unique simply because all of our circumstances are unique.

No extraordinary childhood illnesses, no near brushes with death, or sudden wealth or fame. Just another story of a young boy, growing into being a young man, and then an adult, one moment at a time.

Justin's Dad was a traveling salesman, and was typically gone for three weeks out of the month. The relationship between Justin and his dad was performance driven; if young Justin did the expected thing with excellence, it was acknowledged. If the effort was anything less than that, it was scorned, scolded, or ignored. So affirmation from his father was always for something that he did; never for "who he was."

Growing up, it never occurred to Justin that there was anything abnormal in his relationship with his father. It simply was what it was. His mother unwittingly put Justin in an abnormal mother-son relationship by leaning on him for some of the emotional support she was missing from her husband. "I found myself in the role of a piece maker and comforter with my Mom. Justin reflected, It was natural, because I was the oldest and my Dad was gone so much."

An average student in school, Justin chose not to go to college but to simply get a job. He started in retail, and worked his way to an assistant manger role in a family owned market. From there he went to one of the area's largest employers and worked in production for a year. He had once asked a man at church if he had any positions open at his construction firm, and it was a surprise when one day the man called Justin 4 years after the request, and offered him a job as an apprentice.

Timing and circumstance can sometimes only be appreciated in hindsight, but this was truly a life changing moment. Well, maybe life changing is a bit strong, but career changing at the least. After six years with the company, Justin, now a full fledged journeyman, took a job as an independent contractor for a firm that distributed large farm implements. Within a couple of years Justin had developed a department for the company, complete with a couple of employees, and a self supporting infrastructure. Thinking to himself that perhaps he could start his own company and perhaps have his current employer as a customer, he told his boss about his idea. His boss said; "go ahead, you're on your own; but don't count on us!"

With no other option but to succeed, Justin has put together a nice business. In less than six years, it has turned from a dream, to a reality. He has a strong company in a less than robust economy. Truly, he has been blessed.

As is always the case; there is more to the story. Two major things need to be added to set the stage for my opening paragraph. Remember that I was talking about February 19, 2009 as a line-in-the-sand moment? What would prompt such a time?

One component is Justin's personal life above the waterline. The other is the part that is below it. Wouldn't you know it!

Go back with me if you will to Justin as a young man. One day in church a new family came in that had a daughter named Sue. A couple of years younger than Justin, she immediately caught his eye and a dating relationship ensued. It was really and truly the only relationship either one had. High school sweethearts, they married when Justin was 23 and Sue was 20. Justin fit in well with Sue's family and they started married life in what seemed like a healthy normal way. Children came, and responsibilities grew. The American dream playing itself out again on their own stage.

Go back even further too when Justin was 11 or 12. A friend of his showed Justin his Dad's stash of Playboy's and Penthouses! No big deal. Every young boys dream; right? And so very innocently, it began. Sneaking looks at the magazines whenever a chance allowed turned into buying them when opportunity came. Along with the magazines came the desire to give in to the lust he was feeding. Justin did what many consider to be normal and healthy for an unmarried young boy; he relieved his sexual desires with self gratification.

As he got older, he would get the occasional movie. Later would come the occasional visit to a strip club. Then later still the internet; my goodness, it began to spiral out of control. Until it happened. The thing that will always happen at some point sooner or later. Justin's secret world, got revealed.

Let me back up a bit. Why didn't Justin quit that stuff once he got married? Wouldn't most guys simply say; ok, time to put all of that away? Hmmmm. In talking with Justin, he told me that's exactly what he tried to do; but it only had short term success. How come?

The short answer is that sin, left unchecked, left unaccounted for, grows. In particular, the type of sin that we would prefer to keep secret. And so it is with pornography. Perhaps the biggest temptation facing modern man. With access to all and any kind of temptation a person can want, within the click of a mouse on the Internet, temptation is not only always present, it's omnipresent. And so it's easy to for us to stray in that dark underworld with no physical evidence apparent.

As we know however, that's not quite true. And when subtle signs begin to reveal themselves to those that are closest to us, the damn breaks, and the floodwaters escape.

The intimacy that is shared between a husband and wife can and should be a wonderful expression of their love and commitment. God has wired us to enjoy that expression, and he also has given us a "drive" in that area that needs healthy boundaries.

When those boundaries are already compromised at a young age by viewing inappropriate material, and going to questionable places, it becomes a cancer on the soul. Left unchecked, it will continue to grow until it is obvious to all that something is wrong.

So it happened for Justin. Just like Paul in Romans 7: 18b - 20 *"For I have the desire to do what is good, but I cannot carry it out. For what I do is not the good I want to do; no, the evil I want to do – this I keep on doing. Now if I do what I do not want to do, it is no longer I who do it; but it is sin living in me that does it."*

Wow! Read that a couple of times and let it sink in. Does something make sense to you in all of this? For me, I told myself hundreds of times I wouldn't stop at the party store for alcohol; sometimes within seconds before I actually went in and bought some anyways. What's up with that? It's sin, acting independently of our free will, finding and choosing it's own course.

So how do we fight this sin our life? How did Justin deal with it once it became apparent he could not do it in his own strength?

Well first it has to be identified. Occasionally that happens through self-examination, but often it gets revealed through unpleasant and embarrassing circumstances, that we (at least at the time), would just as soon did not happen. So it was for Justin.

The first time Sue knew he had a problem was about 5 years into their marriage. Justin tells me the story:

"It's almost like I wanted to get caught. He explained. I was so sick of the hidden life style, but it kept getting bigger and bigger. I had visited some pornographic web sites and somehow accidently it became our home page. The next time Sue logged in, there it was."

Sue was devastated. The man she had put on a bit of a pedestal, had come crashing down. Hurt, betrayal, confusion, and anger were all real emotions that surfaced over the next several weeks.

Justin continued his story. "I was actually relieved, he told me. I figured with it being out in the open, my temptation would stop, and I wouldn't struggle with it anymore. And so I made commitments and promises to Sue that I was sincere about, but over time was unable to keep."

What is it in our humanity that makes us think that we can do it alone? Pride is one reason to be sure, shame would be another. So Justin experienced what countless others have experienced when trying to do the battle of life alone. It doesn't work.

I asked Justin if he sought help from the Lord during this time of continuing struggle. "I did! He exclaimed. But it never seemed to be enough, I was beginning to think I would never have victory over this problem."

As time went on, the exposure of "slips" in Justin's addiction began to take it's toll on their marriage. It finally got to a crisis point where Sue told him he needed to move out and get himself fixed. "I was so confused Tom, he told me. I thought these kind of addictions didn't happen to middle class, ordinary people like myself; boy was I wrong!"

So Justin left the house and got a cot and slept at the office for several nights. Knowing that he had to do something different then what he had been trying, he went to a local family counseling ministry that referred him to an individual in the community that had overcome a similar story. When Justin met Bruce for coffee, it was the start of a long road back.

That meeting introduced Justin to the group "Finishing Strong" that I am also a member of. A group of individuals dedicated to finishing the life we have been granted yet here on this earth, with integrity, and conformation of us to be like Christ.

But a lot of trust had been broken. In those early days of intentional, deliberate recovery, Justin needed to humble himself in many ways. He agreed to take lie detector tests to prove his sincerity. He established a policy of not carrying cash with him so that he couldn't easily buy or rent pornographic material. He created an individual accountability relationship with Ken, another man in this book, and a key member of our Finishing Strong group. Justin also started and has continued counseling with an accredited counselor who has expertise in this area. He shares his experiences, strengths, weaknesses, hope, and concern freely with his wife, his accountability partner, his group, his counselor, and most importantly with God.

That brings us back to the beginning. To that Thursday in February where he rededicated his life to Christ. Where he decided to draw a line in the sand and commit to honesty and integrity over these vulnerable areas that he had struggled so many years with. So what kind of an impact does this decision of Justin's make?

It's huge. As trust grows back in his marriage, intimacy starts to grow. Trusting God helps create intimacy with God, and the people close to you in life. All of this is a key component to long term recovery. The home life becomes a more comfortable place for his children to be. To know you are accepted by *grace,* regardless of your performance; well the sky becomes the limit.

Sue and Justin recently adopted a young son from Africa and the opportunity to influence his life in a positive way would not have come unless Justin had made this decision. He makes a positive impact in our group, and with his employees, and as he has opportunity to share his journey with others that may struggle, he begins to influence lives for God's kingdom.

A moment in time came where Justin knew something had to change. It wasn't a nano second, or even a specific hour in a specific day. But like the great divide high up in the Canadian Rockies, there is a point where the water separates and flows into different oceans. One is the sea of life, the other the sea of death. Justin chose life.

Chapter 16

"Brendan Manning"

*"Are you not done tormenting me with your accursed time!
It's abominable! When! When! One day, is that not enough
for you, one day he went dumb, one day I went blind, one day
we'll go deaf, one day we were born, one day we shall die,
the same day, the same second, is that not enough for you?"*

by
Samuel Beckett

Have you ever had a day like that? Or perhaps a season of
your life? I have. And I know that the man I am writing
about now has had them also. And, very selfishly, I'm glad
he did, because it helped shape him, and mold him into the
man he became. And then he took those experiences and
wrote about them, and talked about how to get victory over
those dark days, and bask in the redemptive power of our
God; not easy work, but so available for those who will put
their trust in him. And he gave me those words and insights
at a time where I very badly needed to hear those words, and
experience God's unconditional love.

My first exposure to Brendan Manning was in the early
winter of 2005. It was at a pretty low moment in my life. I
had just agreed to go into alcohol re-hab for the first time in
my life, and try to get a handle on a problem that had plagued
me all of my adult life. I was lost, confused, hurt, and my
spirits were at an all time low. Clearly, it would take God's
define intervention to bring healing.

And that's exactly what happened. I have chronicled my journey in recovery in much greater detail in my first book "Finishing Strong," but suffice it to say that a number of "God moments" happened during that time, that made my recovery possible. I don't know if there is one thing, or one influence that stands above the others, but certainly being introduced to the writings of Brendan Manning stand high on that list. I was given a copy of his book *"Abba's Child"* my first week there, and I have never been the same since.

Born in depression era New York City, Brennan was raised in a Catholic home, attended St. John's University, and after two years there enlisted in the U.S. Marines and went overseas to fight in the Korean War. Upon his return, he went to the University of Missouri to study journalism, but after a semester, dropped out to find something "more" in life.

"Maybe that something "more" is God," an advisor suggested, which triggered Manning to enroll in a Catholic seminary in Loretto, Pennsylvania.

Manning picks up his story; he writes: *"On February 8, 1956, in a little chapel in Loretto, Pennsylvania, I was ambushed by Jesus of Nazareth. The road I've traveled since then is pockmarked by disastrous victories and magnificent defeats, soul-diminishing successes and life-enhancing failures. Seasons of fidelity and betrayal, periods of consolation and desolation, zeal and apathy are not unknown to me. And there have been times...*

when the felt presence of God was more real to me than the chair I am sitting on;

when the Word ricocheted like broken-back lightning in
every corner of my soul;
when a storm of desire carried me to places I have never
visited.
And there have been other times…
when the fire in my belly flickered and died;
when I mistook dried-up enthusiasm for gray-haired wisdom;
when I dismissed youthful idealism as mere naiveté;
when I preferred cheap slivers of glass to the pearl of great
price."

Brennan, is a man who has journeyed lives highways and byways. As a young priest he sought out poverty and recluse in effort to more fully understand, experience, and see God. He started and expanded ministries among the poor and down-trodden in several different places around the world. He battled alcoholism, and nearly died to the disease. He fought his way back through that, through depression, and experienced God's grace when he thought he was truly unworthy. And so much of his writing is geared to this: the fact that it is not by our acts, but it is by grace we are saved.

In his book *"Abba's Child"* Manning writes:

"One of the most shocking things in the American Church is the intense dislike many followers of Jesus have for themselves. They are more displeased with their own short-comings than they ever would dream of being with someone else's. They are sick of their own mediocrity and disgusted with their own inconsistency."

Quoting David Seamunds, Brennan further writes:

"Many Christians find themselves defeated by the most psychological weapon that Satan uses against them. That weapon? Low self-esteem. Satan's greatest psychological weapon is a gut level feeling of inferiority, inadequacy, and low self-worth. This feeling shackles many Christians, in spite of wonderful spiritual experiences and knowledge of God's word. Although they understand their position as sons and daughters of God, they are tied up in knots, bound by a terrible feeling of inferiority, and chained to a deep sense of worthlessness."

Much of Manning's work revolves around the central theme of not buying into the lie that our life, and our circumstances, are uniquely un-qualified for God's unconditional love. And so he weaves a tapestry of stories and short vignettes that rebuke those lies and allow the reader to accept the truth of God's undying grace. And for many Christians and non-Christians alike, that is a very difficult truth to believe in. And so he takes us slowly through his and our wounds, and doubts, and fears, and replaces it with truth, and grace, light, and hope.

See if this passage resonates with you. Again, Manning: *" It used to be that I never felt safe with myself unless I was performing flawlessly. My desire to be perfect had transcended my desire for God. Tyrannized by an all-or-nothing mentality, I interpreted weakness as mediocrity and inconsistency as loss of nerve. I dismissed compassion and self-acceptance as inappropriate responses. My jaded perception of personal failure and inadequacy led to a loss of self-esteem, triggering episodes of mild depression and heavy anxiety."*

So what do you think would be a normal response mechanism to those type of feelings? Perhaps one might try to find the root cause, and seek counseling or professional help, but for most people they would either bury those feelings, or begin to isolate, or perhaps run away from God, or medicate in some way. And perhaps a combination of all of the above without even consciously realizing why they are doing it.

The purpose of this particular book was to describe the series of events that brought a person to Christ, and the type of impact that decision had on others. With Brennan Manning I can't seem to escape talking about his deep struggles with his inner demons, and the painfully slow at times escape out of that deep abyss. Because that's what it is for some of us. A long, slow, painful journey.

As I have mentioned, Brennan has spent much of his life studying, and surrounding and ministering to those individuals that live on the margins. You know who I mean. Some of these people have lost all hope, but for those that have found and received Christ, their walk with God often seems much more serene then most of us. Individuals that are truly happy when they get a warm meal or a dry place to sleep, because it doesn't happen for them all that often. We (I speak for myself now), have a much more difficult time with it all because we have so much that gets in the way. Brennan tells a story in his book *"Ruthless Trust"* that illustrates my point.

"Fourteenth century theologian and mystic John Tauler prayed for eight years that God would bring him a person who would teach him the true way of perfection. One day, while at prayer, he heard a voice from within telling him to

109

go outside to the steps of the church, and there he would meet his mentor. He obeyed without hesitation. On the church steps he found a barefoot man clothed in rags, wounded, and caked with blood."

Tauler greeted the man cordially: "Good morning, dear brother. May God give you a good day, and grant you a happy life."

"Sir, replied the man, I do not ever remember having had a bad day." Stunned, Tauler asked him how that was possible, since sadness and grief are part of the human condition.

The man explained, "You wished me a good day, and I replied that I cannot recall ever having spent a bad day. You see, whether my stomach is full or I am famished with hunger, I praise the Lord equally, when I am rebuffed and despised, I still thank God. My trust in God's providence and his plan for my life is absolute, so there is no such thing as a bad day."

He continued, "Sir, you also wished me a happy life. I must insist that I am always happy for it would be untruthful to state otherwise. My experience of god has taught me that whatever he does must of necessity be good. Thus, everything that I receive from his loving hand or whatever he allows me to receive from the hand of others: be it prosperity or adversity, sweet or bitter: I accept with joy and see it as a sign of his favor. For many, many years now, my first resolution each morning is to attach myself to nothing but the will of God alone. I have learned that the will of God is the love of God. And by the outpouring of his grace, I have so merged my will with his that whatever he wills, I will too. Therefore, I have always been happy."

Well friends, I'm a long ways away from that place. And it's hard for me to even comprehend that I can get to such a place and walk with God as the man at the church's steps did, in my human condition. But when I go back to the question "Am I comfortable with who I am, and whom I am trying to be," and then I reflect on this particular individual from long ago, I realize I have a lot to learn, and a lot to surrender.

Brennan Manning has seen and felt and suffered much. But he also has experienced the pure joy of being in a redeemed relationship with Jesus Christ, and he shares all of that and more with us in his many published works. Thank-you Brennan, for being there when I really needed you. And for you being there again for me today as I reflect on your work, and try to organize a message of hope for those that might read what I have written. I look forward to meeting you some day in glory.

Chapter 17

"Tom"

*"Time is the most un-definable yet paradoxical of things;
The past is gone, the future is not come, and the present
becomes the past even while we attempt to define it, and like
the flash of lightning, it at once exists and expires."*

Charles Colton

The Tom in this story is me. I've told my story in much greater detail in my first book *"Finishing Strong."* In it, I chronicled my journey from a young boy to a middle aged man, struggling to find my identity and value.

While many of the biographies in this book show a very sharply defined moment in time where a significant change occurred in the principle characters life, most of them also show a period of time where seeds were being planted, and lessons were being learned. Certainly, that is the case with me: it just so happens that the "lessons learned" period stretched out much further than I would have cared for, but then again, I need to trust that it was exactly right.

It does little good to second guess and bemoan the fact that lots of mistakes were made, and lots of opportunities were wasted. The only value to going back there at all is to recognize that the hard lessons I've already learned, I need not go through that pain again, and to use it as a tool to help myself and others grow.

<>

What was it that caused me to struggle so much to find my identity and value? I wish I had a good answer for that, I can only say that the struggle was real, and the pain ran pretty deep at times.

I do believe that some of it is just my own unique wiring, the DNA that makes up who I am. An inability to focus as a young boy and man translated into a person that struggled to fit in and find his niche in home, school, and as I got older, general social circles. It took many years, battles with inner demons and addictions, hard life lessons, broken relationships, and times of hopelessness that brought me to a place where I began to learn of another way to live. And even then the lessons came slow; sometimes set aside; and then revelation again.

And I was a person who had things on my side; a strong family network, friends that didn't cast me aside, children that still loved me, a good career, what about those individuals that don't have those assets?

Life is all about relationships. Our walk with God, our journey through life's ups and downs is material only in their relevance to how they shaped us to carry out the relationships we have encountered along the way. God will shape and mold us in our relationships if we are conscious of seeking his will, and being very careful not to manipulate it.

That still remains one of my greatest struggles, seeking the will of God without putting my own personal spin on it.

Sometimes that line can be a little vague, so how do we know? This book wasn't necessarily written to answer that question, but it is the question that comes up again and again in our lives at "moments in time;" and it either gets answered, or ignored, or tabled, or massaged; but the question never just goes away.

<>

I remember being in the bottom bunk in the upstairs bedroom I shared with my brothers Brian and Jeff, I must have been about 9 or 10, and my nightly prayer was troubling:

Now I lay me down to sleep,
I pray the Lord my soul to keep,
If I die before I wake,
I pray the Lord my soul to take.
Amen.

I remember asking my Dad what my soul was, and what happened to my body if I died, and not feeling like I got a very good answer to my question. I remember a number of nights where I was convinced I wouldn't wake up, and I was terrified of the consequences.

Looking back on it, I think there are prayers better suited for a young child, thinking and praying about potential death is probably not the greatest thing for a fairly young mind right before they fall to sleep; and yet, when is the right time to introduce a child to that reality? All I know is that I felt unprepared for that event, and in many respects I still am unprepared today.

When I look back on the landscape of my life, a see a picture that is getting fuller and fuller, but there are clouds in the sky that obscure some of the painting, and there are curves in the road that I can't quite see around; both looking back and forward.

The dream and vision that I constantly look back to and play out in my minds eye is a journey through a large woods. I'm walking along a trail that has many small and some large paths. Some have had dead ends, and I've turned back. Others have taken me quite a long ways away from the main trail; others are quite worn, and some have been barely discernable amongst the deep underbrush. But always I've at least sensed light filtering through the tops of the trees, and sometimes, I've stepped into clearings where the bask of sun was powerful and invigorating, and gave me the energy to keep moving on. Not always knowing what was around the next bend, or over the crest of the next hill, and yet always hope, and faith.

And there are scary animals, and evil people lurking in the shadows: but still the path is always there, never fully obscured. I know and sense a large sunlit meadow once the woods is clear, with a large pristine lake beyond the meadow with white sandy beaches and beautiful ships, and the horizon is clear and bright, near yet far, just a bit out of reach. I see and live my dream in those woods, but they no longer frighten me. I see them instead as a place of opportunity where I might meet friends and others that may wish to walk the path with me. The journey seems much brighter these days. I'm clearly going in the right direction.

And yet, the right path is not always perfectly clear, but the wrong path is quickly evident when we are in a right relationship with God. So sometimes I believe we are asked to be still and wait; perhaps sitting underneath a tree and waiting for the sun to come up and help guide our way, sometimes it stays night for a long time. It depends on the season of life as well, and the heart of the traveler.

Does all of that make sense to you? If it does, then I believe you also have learned a lot about life's journey, and yet you recognize that the journey is never really over. It's the Christian life! Wonderfully profound and utterly simple all in the same breath.

I'm writing about myself in February of 2010, age 55, single, content and restless at the same time. I am experiencing the moment better than I used to, but still a long way's from where I would like it to be. How do I know that? The evidence is found in a lot of little things, and some big things if I am tuned in to my spirit. And I can't do that unless I am intentional about certain things. Let me expand on that thought.

It's very difficult for me to appreciate what I'm feeling unless I'm intentional about the discovery process. And the discovery process has a number of different elements associated to it. There is my prayer and devotional life, there is self discovery, there is an openness to input from others, there is taking the time to engage with other individuals that may battle some of the same things you do, and there is seeking out professional help when you're not sure which way to look for answers. All of those are important elements and considerations for me to stay healthy today.

And I need to feel and experience success. Part of "walk through the woods" is knowing that you are going in the right direction; and that gets validated in different ways. A comfort with who you are, a quiet satisfaction on a goal accomplished without fanfare, affirmation from friends and loved ones, the list goes on.

And so I journey, and I understand more and less simultaneously; a paradox; mixed metaphors to be sure, but it makes sense to me.

The Tom I am is the sum of my experiences. The Tom I wish to be can only be realized by walking in the light today, as best I know it. I thank God for making me finally see the truth of that simplicity. May I hold on to it.

Chapter 18

"Under The Water Line"
&
"The Story of the Red Lizard"

*"There are whole years for which I hope I will never be
cross-examined, for I could not give an alibi."*

by
Mignon McLaughlin

An iceberg has over 90% of its mass under the water line.
The 10% that is above the water line is what is visible to the
casual observer. And aren't most of us like that as well? We
don't have to scratch much below the surface in most people
to discover that there is a lot more to them then what you
might first observe – good or bad. It's the stuff "under the
water line" that doesn't get talked about, or revealed until
something causes what is down below to surface and expose
itself.

Sometimes, it's not so much what is under the water line
revealing itself as something or someone getting to close to
what is above the water line and subsequently getting
damaged. Does that make sense? When a ship hits an
iceberg, the damage is typically done below the water line on
the ship with what is below the water line on the iceberg. So
often this is true in human relationships as well.

Often, we find out through circumstance that we had no idea
a person was like this; or that. How often haven't we heard
the story on the evening news that so and so went ballistic

and went into the cafeteria and just randomly starting shooting people. But when the investigation starts to take place, it is discovered that there was all manner of dysfunction in that person's life, but it either wasn't recognized, or it was ignored.

And when we find out about stuff that most people don't know about, its usually negative stuff, rarely is an individual hiding or trying to control some of their character strengths and attributes. No, they hide their flaws and weaknesses.

Why am I bringing this up now? How is this relevant to the whole subject of "A Moment in Time?"

Tiger Woods, the consummate athlete, arguably the greatest golfer who ever played the game, is an interesting example of being an individual that has and had a lot of "stuff" under the water line. And until that "stuff" is examined and dealt with in a healthy way, the amount we have below the water line gets bigger and bigger, more heavy all the time.

As I am writing in this chapter in the early days of December 2009, Tigers world is unraveling. His carefully controlled public image has been brutally massacred by his clandesent relationships with a number of different women.

We had the life that Tiger allowed us to see. The on the golf course player, the interviews in the press tent, and statements on his web site, and the occasional talk show. Other than that, he tried to shroud himself in privacy, and put things in place that would keep others from getting to near him. A lot of that is understandable.

But what happens when we do that over long periods of time? Habits develop that typically are not healthy. Lacking accountability, we twist into our own selfish world and "feed the pig" until it becomes too big to ignore and you realize you have a hog in the room. All devouring. All consuming.

And that keeps us from getting healthy and allowing the spirit of truth and the Lord from entering our life. As long as so much of us remains hidden: sometimes even from *ourselves*, it is very difficult to have the spirit of reconciliation and rebirth the opportunity it so needs to allow us to be "born again."

And so we would see glimpses of the under the waterline personality of Tiger on the course. Uncontrolled anger and frustration at bad shots. A propensity to lose control when a fan would snap the camera at an inopportune moment. Evidence of something within that wasn't being dealt with in a healthy way.

Now I'm not a psychologist, but I know enough about recovery to recognize a few things. When you have unresolved issues in your life, the tendency is to medicate. And you usually choose things that will give you instant gratification, not long term peace. So things like sex, and alcohol, and drugs, and money, and power all become very alluring. And they work for a moment. But then shame and guilt set in and the cure becomes more medication, so the cycle continues until we don't know how to stop it in our own power. And the truth is we can't.

Eventually, the truth of our secret world, the stuff under the water line gets exposed. And when it does, everyone is amazed at the size of it! Including ourselves. So it was no big surprise to me when the first glimpse at Tiger's problems (the simple little car accident), opened the floodgates for all kinds of dysfunction being revealed. It's a timeless story, repeated over and over again.

<>

I am reprinting the story of the "Red Lizard," from C.S. Lewis's *"The Great Divorce"* as a wonderful allegory of what it looks like when we rid ourselves of our demons and that part of us that is lurking unseen below sea level. Read it carefully.

"The Story of the Little Red Lizard"
by
C.S. Lewis from *"The Great Divorce"*

(A dream where residents of hell (sort of) have taken a bus ride into the foothills of heaven (or something close to it) to "check it out", criticize, argue, return—or perhaps stay and become like "angels" Our narrator (an interested observer) stumbles across the following scene.)

..I saw coming towards us a Ghost (a visitor from "hell") who carried *something* on his shoulder. Like all the Ghosts, he was insubstantial, but they differed from one another as smokes differ. Some had been whitish; this one was dark and oily.

What sat on his shoulder was a *little red lizard,* and it was twitching his tail like a whip and whispering things in his ear. As I caught sight of him he turned his head to the reptile with a snarl of impatience.

"Shut up, I tell you!" he said. It wagged his tail and continued to whisper to him. He (the ghost) ceased snarling, and presently began to smile. Then he turned and began to limp westward, away from the mountains ("heaven").

"Off so soon?" said a voice. The speaker was more or less human in shape but larger than a man, and so bright I could hardly stand to look at him. His presence smote on my eyes and on my body too (for there was heat coming from him as well as light) like the morning sun at the beginning of a tyrannous summer day.

"Yes I'm off," said the Ghost. "Thanks for all your hospitality. But it's no good, you see. I told this little chap," (here he indicated the lizard), "that he'd have to be quiet if he came—which he insisted on doing. Of course his stuff won't do here: I realize that. But he won't stop. I shall just have to go home."

"Would you like me to make him quiet?" said the flaming Spirit—an angel, as I now understood.

"Of course I would," said the Ghost.

"Then I will kill him," said the Angel, taking a step forward.

"Oh—ah—look out! You're burning me! Keep away," said the Ghost, retreating.

"Don't you *want* him killed?" Said the Angel.

"You didn't say anything about *killing* him at first," replied the Ghost. "I hardly meant to bother you with anything as drastic as that."

"It's the only way," said the Angel, taking a step forward. "So, shall I kill it?"

"Well that's a further question," mused the Ghost, I'm quite open to consider it, but it's a new point, isn't it? I mean, for the moment I was only thinking about silencing it because up here—well, it's so damn embarrassing."

"May I kill it?"

"Well there is time to discuss that later."

"There is no time. May I kill it?"

"Please, I never meant to be such a nuisance. Please— really—don't bother. Look! It's gone to sleep of it's own accord! I'm sure it'll be all right now. Thanks ever so much."

"May I kill it?"

"Honestly, I don't think there is the slightest necessity for that. I'm sure I shall be able to keep it in order now. I think the gradual process would be far better than killing it."

"The gradual process is of no use at all," said the Angel.

"Don't you think so?" Quickly replied the Ghost. "Well, I'll think over what you have said very carefully. I honestly will. In fact, I'd let you kill it now, but as a matter of fact I'm not feeling frightfully well today. It would be silly to do it *now.* I'd need to be in good health for the operation. Some other day, perhaps.

"There is no other day. All days are present now."

"Get back! You're burning me. How can I tell you to kill it? You'd kill *me* if you did."

"It is not so," said the Angel.

"Why, your hurting me now," relied the Ghost.

"I never said it wouldn't hurt you, I said it wouldn't kill you."

"Oh, I know. You think I'm a coward. But it isn't that. Really it isn't. I say! Let me run back by tonight's bus and get an opinion from my own doctor. I'll come again the first minute I can."

"This moment contains all moments," said the Angel somberly.

"Oh why are you torturing me? You are jeering at me. How *can* I let you tear me to pieces. If you wanted to help me, why didn't you kill the damn thing without asking me—before I knew? It would have been all over by now if you had."

"I can not kill it against your will. It is impossible. Have I your permission?"

"The angels hands were almost closed on the Lizard, but not quite. Then the Lizard began chattering to the Ghost so loud that even I could hear what it was saying.

"Be careful," it said. "He can do what he says. He can kill me. One fatal word from you and he *will*! Then you'll be without me for ever and ever. It's not natural. How could you live? You'd only be a sort of ghost, not a real man as you are now. He doesn't understand. It may be natural for him, but it isn't for us. Yes, yes. I know there are no real pleasures now, only dreams. But aren't they better than nothing? And I'll be so good. I admit I've sometimes gone to far in the past, but I *promise* I won't do it again. I'll give you nothing but really nice dreams—all sweet and fresh and almost innocent..."

"Have I you permission?" Said the Angel to the Ghost.

"I know it will kill me."

"It won't. But supposing it did?"

"You're right. I would be better to be dead than to live with this creature."

"Then I may?"

"Damn and blast you! Go on, get it over. Do what you like," bellowed the Ghost: but ended whimpering, "God help me. God help me."

The next moment the ghost gave a scream of agony such as I have never heard on earth. The Burning One closed his crimson grip on the reptile: twisted it, while it bit and writhed, and then flung it, broken backed, on the turf.

"Ow! That's done for me," gasped the Ghost, reeling backwards.

For a moment I could make out nothing distinctly. Then I saw, between me and the nearest bush, unmistakably solid, but growing every minute more solid, the upper arm and shoulder of a man. Then brighter and still stronger, the legs and hands. The neck and head materialized while I watched...the actual completing of a man—an immense man, naked, not much smaller than the Angel.

What distracted me was at the same time something seemed to be happening to the Lizard. At first I thought the operation had failed. Far from dying, the creature was still struggling and growing bigger as it struggled. And as it grew, it changed. It's hinder parts grew rounder. The tail, still flickering, became a tail of hair that flickered between huge and glossy buttocks. Suddenly, I started back, rubbing my eyes. What stood before me was the greatest stallion I had ever seen, silvery white but with a mane and tail of gold. It was smooth and shining, rippled with swells of flesh and muscle, whinnying and stamping with it's hoofs. At each stamp of his mighty hoofs the land and trees shook and trembled.

The new-made man turned and clapped the new hoses neck. It nosed his bright body. Horse and master breathed each into the other's nostrils. The man turned from it, flung himself at the feet of the Burning One, and embraced them. When he rose I thought his face shone with tears, but it may have only been the liquid love and brightness (one can not distinguish them in that country) which flowed from him. I had not long to think about it. In joyous haste the young man leaped upon the horses back. Turning in his seat he waved a farewell, then nudged the stallion with his heals. They were off before I knew what was happening. There was riding if you like! I came out as quickly as I could from among the bushes to follow them with my eyes; but already they were only like a shooting star far off on the green plain, and soon among the foothills of the mountains. Then, still like a star, I saw them winding up, scaling which seemed impossible steeps, and quicker every moment, till near the dim brow of the landscape, so high that I must strain my neck to see them, they vanished, bright themselves into the rose-brightness of that everlasting morning.

While I still watched, I noticed that the whole plain and forest were shaking with a sound which in our world would be too large to hear, but there I could take it with joy. I know it was not the solid people who were singing. It was the voice of the earth, those woods and those waters. A strange archaic, inorganic noise, that came from all directions at once. It sang,

"The master says to our master, Come up. Share my rest and splendor till all natures that were your enemies become slaves to dance for you.."

"From beyond all place and time, out of the very place, authority will be given unto you: the strengths that once opposed you shall be obedient fire in your blood and thunder in your voice." "overcome us that, so overcome, we may be ourselves: we desire the beginning of your reign as we desire dawn and dew, wetness at the birth of light."

Is there a take away for you in that story? Time stands still for there is only now. Will you cast your burdens and sin aside and let the Burning One transform you into a new man? Will you let your greatest weakness become your greatest strength? Will you give up your will and change from the man that was ready to limp back to the bus, to the man that leaped upon the stallions back? Those are the questions I had to ask myself at a point in my life, and it wasn't easy to allow the Burning One to grasp the lizard from me. And there was pain when he did. But from that point, I began to grow. And although naked at first, I was given what I needed for the day I was in. One day at a time; one moment at a time.

This is a powerful story, with a powerful message. But in the end, it's only that; a story. We, you and I have the opportunity to create our own story, in which we can do no more than live in the moment of time we are in. That is the truth of life that must never escape us.

And so I close this chapter with simple thoughts and words. A poem I've crafted to illustrate the point I tried to make. Take from it what you will; and leave the rest.

A Moment in Time

Nothing new
Under the sun
Everything I've thought
It seems that it's done

I tried recapturing youth
But when I was done
I discovered wasted moments
Chasing things I called fun

Watershed moments
I've had a few
I'll transfer that knowledge
From me, unto you

It's been through pain
That most of my lessons, I've learned
Seldom on sunny days
But on dark ones, I've heard

The call of God's voice
When in silence I'd hear
"My son, listen closely
You have nothing to fear"

So stumbling forward
With God by my side
I look for his will
And swallow my pride

Each day much the same
Yet all incredibly different
Teach, grow, and stretch me
To be God's humble, servant

And all of this happens
Surreal, and sublime
All with God's leading
A moment in time

Chapter 19

"Full Circle"

"The only reason for time is so that everything doesn't happen at once."

by
Albert Einstein

If you remember, in my introduction I mention the seed that was planted that caused me to start thinking about writing this book. The idea is that we influence individuals within our small sphere of influence, and then they do the same, and on and on.

In a complex set of gears, a small drive gear can wind up moving mammoth gears and loads. There is an old axiom; "give me a large enough lever, and I can move the earth." I have tried in this book to connect some of those gears and axiom's that I have observed in my study and in my personal life. One the one hand, I don't feel that I am any further ahead then I was when I started. If anything, the whole elusive understanding of time is less clear than when I began. On the other, I am somewhat comforted by the fact that no one really seems to have a clear definition, other than God, and I have begun to believe that he wants it that way.

But do we have a responsibility to use our influence, the things that we have learned, to do God's good and perfect will? I believe the answer is "absolutely." In first Corinthians 12, Paul talks about spiritual gifts, and the fact that we are all blessed differently: and so some may teach, or build, or tend to the sick, or become missionaries – the list goes on. But the point is made: "we are all one body" (1st Corinthians 12: verse 12 paraphrased).

In second Corinthians 9: verse 13 Paul writes: *"Because of the service by which you have proved yourselves, men will praise God for the obedience that accompanies your confession of the gospel of Christ, and for your generosity in sharing with them and with everyone else."*

And in Hebrews 10: verse 24 *"And let us consider how we may spur each other on toward love and good deeds."*

These are just a couple of examples of where God's word instructs and urges us to use our gifts to advance the kingdom of Christ, and have his will live through us. It's a lifelong commission and our call as followers of Christ.

Another question I asked was: "Are you comfortable with who you are, and who you want to be?"

I think it is a question that one should ask him or herself often, in a very real sense it is a petition to God himself. When the psalmist writes in Psalm 139: 23-24 *"Search me O God, and know my heart; try me and know my thoughts: and see if there be any wicked way in me, and lead me in the way everlasting."* Is not David (the psalmist) asking that very question? Perhaps to paraphrase the scripture: "Lord, examine my life, help me in that examination, show me what I should change, so that I may live a life in which I am assured you will be well pleased."

Of course the problem with that is in our human condition we never really quite "get there." And what is that condition known as "there?" Will we ever truly know in this life? Even with our best intentions? So then what?

This book was never intended to really answer that question; it was really just a prompt to perhaps examine your life, as I and countless others have done and continue to do over time. I believe that if you seek the answer to that question, in prayer, meditation, and fellowship, you will be drawn to the resources and the answers. Certainly God's holy word the Bible, is the place to start. And then perhaps some of the writings of individuals I've named in this book ; and countless other resources as well. I'm reminded of a quote from the Greek philosopher Socrates that lived 400 years before Christ that seems to fit this moment: *"The unexamined life is not worth living."*

It was also intended to show how in the lives of different individuals that I've chosen (I certainly could have chosen a lot more!), that undefined length, but certainly real, moments of time came, where their lives changed. And history changed as a result. And there are no insignificant individuals in history; we all have a part in it, whether that part is recognized by many or not. Certainly God recognizes what we did or did not do.

And so I think that is really it. God has blessed mankind with intellect, free will, and the ability to make choices. It's always been that way, and forever it will be. Some are harder than others. Some come quickly, others slowly; but they all happen in; a moment in time.

32,128